SIXTH SENSE

Leading psychic intuitive Sue Bishop appears regularly in the media and at mind, body, spirit festivals. She was featured in the TV documentary, *Everyone's A Psychic*, as well as her own *Psychic Live* shows where she entertains audiences with her sight and insights. Sue is the director of the Chiara College of Metaphysics. As a truly gifted psychic and experienced presenter, Sue knows how to captivate people with her wonderfully down-to-earth, intelligent and lively approach.

SIXTH SENSE

everyday experiences and what they reveal

Sue Bishop

inspired LIVING

ALLEN&UNWIN

Dedicated to Michelle de Souza and my sister Lena Ferraro.

Two bright stars.

First published in 2011

Inspired Living, an imprint of
Allen & Unwin
Sydney, Melbourne, Auckland, London

83 Alexander Street
Crows Nest NSW 2065
Australia
Phone: (61 2) 8425 0100
Fax: (61 2) 9906 2218
Email: info@allenandunwin.com
Web: www.allenandunwin.com

Cataloguing-in-Publication details are available
from the National Library of Australia
www.trove.nla.gov.au

ISBN 978 1 74237 561 8

Set in 12/17 pt Dante MT by Bookhouse, Sydney
Printed in Australia by SOS Print + Media Group

10 9 8

MIX
Paper from responsible sources
FSC® C011217

The paper in this book is FSC® certified.
FSC® promotes environmentally responsible, socially beneficial and economically viable management of the world's forests.

Contents

Acknowledgements viii
Introduction ix

1 Your Sixth Sense 1
2 The Twilight Zone 4
3 Who's Hanging Around? 7
4 Do You See What I See? 10
5 I Just Opened My Eyes 15
6 Whispers in My Ear 18
7 It's What I Feel 21
8 Reaching for the Other Side 25
9 The Thing About Energy 30
10 Reading the Signs 33
11 Activating Your Sixth Sense 36
12 Trust Your Sixth Sense Regardless 39
13 How to See and Feel Energy 42
14 How to Live the High Life 44
15 Creating a Little Magic in Your Life 49

16 Be Careful What You Wish For 53
17 Unleash Your Past 56
18 I Know You 60
19 A Sneak Peek 64
20 I'm Beside Myself 68
21 Frequent Flyers not Required for Where We're Going 72
22 There's no Time Like the Right Time 76
23 Alchemy 80
24 Everyday Miracles 83
25 The Sixth Sense in Future Tense 87
26 It's Called Animal Instinct for a Reason 90
27 When Oscar Tried to Save Nicole 92
28 Getting a Grip 94
29 Keeping Tight with the Boss 98
30 You've got Mind-mail! 101
31 Dream Catcher 106
32 A Sixth Sense of Humour 112
33 The Witching Hour 115
34 When to go Pro 118
35 Be Honest. Am I Totally Nuts? 122
36 Be Home by Midnight 125
37 Chain-rattlers Anonymous 128
38 When Dad Came to Visit 132
39 My Bags are Packed, I'm Ready 135
40 On the Edge of Forever 138
41 When it's Someone Else's Stuff 141
42 Finding the Right Way Home 146
43 They're Here . . . 151
44 Double Or Nothing 155
45 A Walk in the Clouds 159
46 I'm Into You—Really! 162

47	Where are Your Friends When You Need Them?	166
48	Lifting the Veil	169
49	Because We Need Them	174
50	I Could Use a Little TLC	177
51	Ouch! That Hurt!	183
52	When My Guides Stepped In	187
53	Protect Yourself	190
54	Energy Stuff	194
55	I'm Bulletproof	197
56	Don't Forget to Spring Clean	202
57	Heavenly Hot Property	208
58	Thinking You Can't, but You Can	211
59	More Than a Crystal Ball	217
60	Go to It!	223
61	Don't Forget the Frosting	227

Acknowledgements

How do I thank all the special people who have left their mark on my life, especially those who have help make it easier and happier? You guys know who you are! To my kids Tristan and Chiara—wow, we've been through a lot together but like the phoenix we always rise. I'd like to thank Mick and my family—Mum, Frances, Roy and Joe (Lena you already got the bright star award), Jade and Dad, who is in Spirit but always keeping watch over me.

I'd also like to thank Diana O'Shea for all her help with the initial edits and her valuable feedback on the book. Thanks to all of my students for trusting me to guide them. A huge thanks to Michelle and Steve de Souza for always being there for me. Thank you also to my publisher Maggie Hamilton at Allen & Unwin who has fantastic intuition. After all, she was guided by her sixth sense to ask me to write this book!

And finally, to all my helpers in Spirit—thanks for showing me so many wonders.

Introduction

Sometimes things happen in life that we can't explain. Having a premonition or seeing an apparition for the first time are two of those things. A sixth sense experience can be puzzling because what we're experiencing doesn't always fit in nicely with our understanding of life.

The sixth sense is the part of us that helps us to *see* and *know* things that our normal senses cannot possibly pick up. Call it whatever you like—a hunch, intuition (inner-tuition) or psychic ability—the sixth sense is our extra sensory perception of the world. It's a real pity that so many of us doubt, and even block, this wonderful gift. But we do. I feel it's largely because we fear what we don't understand, those things we can't explain. Rather than investing time in trying to explore the wonderful potential held in such moments, we hide them away. And that's such a waste because it's usually the experiences we can't explain that hold the key to a deeper appreciation of life.

Working with your sixth sense can bring you some amazing rewards like ensuring you are at the right place at the right time to get that incredible job. It can help you pick up on a health issue before it gets out of hand and even help you to cross paths with your perfect match.

You've got the sixth sense, so why not use it? I consider it a privilege to be able to help people understand their paranormal experiences and teach them how to work with their beautiful gift of the sixth sense. This book will show you just how easy it is.

1

Your Sixth Sense

Your sixth sense is your extraordinary sensory gift. It wins hands down over your other five senses, yet remains the most under-utilised. That's because we're not taught enough about our sixth sense and what it can do for us. While it's largely associated with the paranormal, the sixth sense can be used in so many ways in our everyday life. Most of us are held back by a lack of faith in our incredible gift. Why not place a little trust in your sixth sense and see what happens?

There are all kinds of ways you can experience your sixth sense—from seeing premonitions to having gut feelings about a situation or an event. Or you may be able to read other people and know what they are going to do or say before they do it. What a truly wonderful gift! Imagine being able to grab little snapshots of the future and then using these insights to make your life a whole lot easier.

Your sixth sense heightens your awareness of what's really going on inside you and around you. It's as if you are standing in the middle of a forest on a foggy winter morning and don't know which way to turn because everything is so hazy. Suddenly the fog lifts and you're able see everything around you with a crisp clearness. That's the beautiful thing about the sixth sense—it reveals things in their true light. But that's not all it can do. By expanding your perception, the sixth sense helps you to make better life choices by giving you an inner knowing of what is right for you.

Close your eyes for a moment and look back to a time in your life when you abandoned cold logic and followed your intuition. You made the right choice, didn't you? The voice of your soul is the one part of you that's never wrong! It doesn't make mistakes because it works with emotional intelligence.

Heartfelt choices come from your inner truth. Your rational mind understands practical matters but doesn't always have the bigger picture in its sight. If someone at work said to you, 'You're never going to get the promotion you want because you haven't got the talent,' would you believe them? Cold logic will naturally highlight all your faults, and you could easily talk yourself out of going for the promotion. But if your soul said, 'This is right for me, I know I can do the job,' then that instinct needs to be honoured because your soul knows your destiny. Trust that your soul will make the best choices for you, especially during life's critical moments.

Try this exercise if you find yourself unable to make important decisions because conflicting thoughts are bouncing through your mind.

Relax and silence your mind until it is completely blank. It may take a few minutes to achieve but once your mind is clear let your soul show you the solution to your problem. Stay open to the impressions you are sensing. Don't immediately discard things because they seem unusual or far-fetched—they may come as a vision, insight or premonition.

Perhaps the greatest gift the sixth sense gives us is the means to reach across the veil of death and reconnect with our loved ones on the other side. Just because someone is in Spirit now doesn't mean they're completely out of the picture. Death doesn't seem so final when you can sit in your living room and reconnect with people you've missed for a very long time. Mediums can help you open the door to the other side. But I'll let you in on a little secret—you don't need to go to a medium to contact your loved ones. You can do this yourself by working with your sixth sense. Imagine making the dearly departed part of your life again. Wouldn't that be fantastic! And what a shame it would be to bury this part of us.

2

The Twilight Zone

Having recently had a close and unsettling encounter with a ghost I decided to get away for a lovely holiday and found myself on the party island of Ios, a tiny two-town island near Santorini in Greece. After a night of drinking too many cocktails I awoke to find many white, transparent, faceless beings standing in front of me. There they were, row after row of beings made out of light, with the wall clearly behind them. I couldn't discern any facial features, only the outline of human bodies. They didn't say anything. They didn't do anything. I woke up my room-mates and asked if they could see anything. No, they couldn't. This didn't help because I could still see the figures as plain as day.

Putting it down to too much partying, I picked up a book and went outside and sat in the small rocky garden to wake myself up. Every five minutes or so I looked up from my novel, and saw these beings still surrounding me. After an hour I crossed the road to a tavern and sat down with my room-mates and ordered breakfast, hoping that a good meal would ground me. Even as I struck up a conversation with the young Swedish couple sitting opposite me, everywhere I turned, everywhere I looked, there they were—row after row of white, faceless beings.

This went on all day. They followed me down the narrow whitewashed streets and into the small shops, silently watching me as I browsed through racks of colourful clothes. Nothing seemed to scare them off, not even the noisy crowd of tourists at the boisterous bar by the beach where I sat and sipped mineral water. I was desperately hoping my faceless army would eventually disappear into thin air. But they didn't. By the end of the day I felt traumatised. I remember walking down the hillside with the red-hued setting sun disappearing behind the sea, and thinking to myself, 'What if they never go away?' The next morning I woke up and they were gone. It had never crossed my mind to speak to them to find out what they wanted.

At the time I just left it as one of those 'twilight moments' and didn't think about it any more. Only the other day Diana, a lovely student of mine, emailed me and asked, 'Who do you think they were?' She surmised that perhaps they were the spirits of the fallen. Many battles had been fought on this tiny island, famous for being the place where the poet Homer spent his final years. Even as late as the sixteenth century countless lives were lost in pirate battles that raged around that part of the Aegean. I agree with Diana and now feel that the faceless souls I saw had all fallen in battle together. They were following me en masse in the hope that I could help them. Sadly, at the time I had no idea how to do so.

In all subsequent experiences with guides or other spirits I have never seen such an army of faceless beings. I believe they were following me because they knew I could see them, and it gave them an acknowledgement that someone knew they were real. I wish now I had stopped to listen to their story.

This experience in Greece was a turning point for me. After this, I became driven to find out how to work with my sixth sense, to get some peace of mind. I was tired of living in the twilight zone. No more ghosts-popping in my house; no more faceless beings closing in on me and freaking me out. I was going to learn about the paranormal. I was going to learn to work with my psychic abilities in the hope it would empower me. And it did.

3

Who's Hanging Around?

Anyone who has had a paranormal experience can appreciate how disturbing such an event can be, especially when you don't know what to expect or what to do. But it doesn't have to be this way. There is so much you can do to create a win-win situation for both you and your ethereal visitors. If you start working with your sixth sense, it will help you realise what is going on around you.

If you feel your home is haunted, it helps to recognise whether there is an actual presence, or whether you are feeling a projection of your own fear. There are different energies out there and they're not all spirits or lost souls. As you read this book you will learn about many different types of energies, what they are, what they mean, how some of them can help you, and how you can help some of them!

But let's say there is a Spirit in your house. How do you know? A lot of my clients talk about feeling a cold pocket of energy in the spot where they think there's some paranormal activity. I agree there is definitely a change in room temperature where lost souls lurk. Hold out your arms, palms up, and feel if there is a pocket of energy that's uncharacteristically cold (check for draughts and things like that first!). If you feel a cold area, the next thing to do is to tune in to the Spirit by letting your feeling-self guide you. Sense if there is a conscious life force present—that's right, lost souls still hold on to their earthly personality. Your ghost has thoughts and feelings, just like you do.

If the 'presence' feels heavy and negative stop what you're doing and call in an expert who knows how to deal with lost souls. Don't let things get out of hand.

A woman named Sarah called for my help only after her own attempts failed. I sat her down on the lounge and asked her to describe exactly what she was sensing.

'Something dark,' she said with trepidation. 'Can you feel it?'

There was no mistaking the heavy presence in the room.

'I thought I was imagining things,' she said. 'But I couldn't shake this feeling that something was watching me. I felt it following me around and it got to the point where it started freaking me out.'

'What have you done about it?' I asked.

'I smudged the house with sage. I read an article that said smudging sage clears negative vibes from a room.'

'It does,' I agreed. 'When you burn sage, an uplifting essence is released which makes it harder for negative energies to hang around. But that doesn't mean it removes everything, especially if the presence happens to be intelligent and mischievous. What happened after you smudged the house?'

'I presumed it had worked so I went to sleep. A few hours later I woke up and felt this invisible force pressing down hard on my chest and I couldn't breathe.'

Sarah's sixth sense had been spot on. There really was a dark presence there. I cleared it away by calling in my angelic helpers to open up a doorway to take the Spirit to its rightful home. Within minutes the atmosphere felt incredibly comfortable.

Trust that your sixth sense will show you what's really hanging around. It will show you the difference between the unsettling energies of a tormented lost soul and the lovely energies of a friendly ghost. Instead of allowing the unknown to push your fear button every time it appears, let your sixth sense tell you if, and when, you need to take action.

Once you understand that your sixth sense equips you to handle extra sensory events like paranormal activity, you're one step closer to mastering your environment.

4

Do You See What I See?

I had one of these moments when I woke up in the middle of the night about twenty-five years ago. I remember it was cold and raining outside as I made my way down the dark hallway towards the bathroom. Suddenly, I was stopped in my tracks. Out of nowhere I felt someone grip my shoulder. I spun around, knowing full well that no one could possibly be there, and froze. An unfathomable 'presence' surrounded me and I instinctively knew it wanted to throw me down the stairs. A raw fear gripped me and I ran back to the comfort of my bed where I huddled up close to my partner and tried to forget what had just happened.

'You're imagining things,' I told myself.

But it happened again the following night, and the night after that. Each night as I approached the small landing near the stairs I felt my invisible intruder waiting for me. I tried to convince myself I was hallucinating but the fear ripping through my body told me it was very real. As the days slipped into months I grew scared to cross that spot even in broad daylight.

Like most people faced with the unexplainable, I kept this secret to myself.

Then things started to get really strange. One day I was sitting alone, drawing in my bedroom when I looked up and saw a man standing on the other side of the room. He had a rough, deeply lined face framed with dark curly hair. He was dressed in old-fashioned clothes. I stared for a few minutes then blinked a few times. Suddenly he disappeared. Would you believe, once again I kept it to myself?

A few days later a watch on top of the dressing table fell to the floor. I stopped what I was doing and stared at where it had landed. There had to be a logical explanation. Ten minutes later a shoe went flying across the room. There was no wind, nothing that could make a shoe move like that. This time, instead of trying to rationalise the experience, I chose to ignore it altogether. Isn't it funny how we can ignore something that doesn't quite fit in with our picture of how things are meant to be?

A few minutes later another object moved. Then another. By now I could no longer ignore things. Something strange was definitely happening—something I couldn't understand and didn't want to understand. All I knew was that I wanted it to stop. A few more objects moved by themselves and then I ran out of the room, down the stairs and out of the house. I barged into the music shop where my partner worked. When he looked up at me all I could say was, 'Ghost!'

To calm me down my partner decided to ask his work colleague Tony for advice on dealing with the ghost. Tony looked him straight in the eye and smiled, 'You need to talk to my ex-wife. She's into all this sort of thing.'

If it hasn't happened to you, trust me—seeing a ghost in your room, feeling them trying to throw you down the stairs, and then watching objects flying around, kind of shakes you up. The hardest thing is fighting the fear and not having any control over the situation. You can imagine my relief when Tony's ex-wife Rhondda turned up on our doorstep.

Rhondda cleared the house by sending the ghost home. She did this by opening a portal to the Spirit world, then she invited angels, Spirit guides and members of this man's family, who were already in Spirit, to come to welcome him back. The spirits assured him that everything was fine and he was finally going home. While I was scared at the time, I've learned since that watching a tormented soul be liberated from the earth plane and find peace and happiness by being reunited with their loved ones is one of the most beautiful sights to watch. This poor man's nightmare had ended. He was no longer stuck in between worlds, lost and alone. He was free to begin the next chapter in his life on the other side with all the love and support he craved.

I was intrigued when Rhondda told me about the life of this man and how he had become a ghost. Apparently he was a dock worker who lived in my house in 1912. One day his little girl begged him for a special present for her birthday. He was too poor to buy her what she wanted but she wouldn't let up and eventually he lost his temper and chased her down the landing. She tripped at the top of the narrow stairs, fell and broke her neck. Hearing all the commotion, the mother came out of the kitchen and discovered her daughter dead on the stairs. Without thinking she ran up and started hitting her husband across the chest. He tried to pull her back so he could explain how the accident happened, but she lost her footing and then she too fell and met her death on the stairs. In that tragic moment the dock worker lost the only two people he had ever loved. And it was his fault. He never forgave himself for their deaths. When he died years later he refused to go to the light—the tunnel of light leading home to the Spirit world—because he thought the angels would send him to hell. Instead of crossing over to the other side, he entered into a nightmare place in the lower astral plane, having a silent existence between worlds where no one could see or hear him. Here he'd recreated his life on earth. In his world it was still 1912, but strangers kept moving into his house and totally ignoring him when he asked them to leave.

Rhondda explained that the man had become increasingly traumatised over the years because no one had validated his existence. Imagine what it must feel like to have everybody constantly ignoring you in your own house. Through Rhondda he asked for help. He said he hadn't been trying to throw me down the stairs, he had only been trying to explain what had happened. He had been trying to communicate in the only way he could, through feelings and sensations. But I hadn't been listening.

He hadn't known he was dead and thought he was in a never-ending dream. Time stops for lost souls. One day stretches for an eternity, until they manage to cross over into the light. Desperate, lonely and angry, he had finally managed to find a way to move objects to draw my attention. It takes an enormous amount of energy and will to move a watch or a shoe when you don't have a physical body, but this poor man had really wanted to escape his nightmare and had hoped I could help him.

He also told Rhondda that I'd drawn a picture about the accident. We hunted around the house and found it. It was a drawing of a mother and her young daughter surrounded by cloudy shadows. The mother had tears in her eyes, holding the young girl in her arms. There was a staircase made of broken bones spiralled around them. I had unconsciously tapped into their story. I had the answer the whole time, and hadn't known it. Like a lot of us my soul was listening, but my head had shut it all out.

Sometimes life throws an unexpected curve ball that makes us question what we know and feel. I like to think of these kinds of experiences as precious opportunities to learn because they inspire us to see our world with new eyes. Being terrorised by a ghost ended up being a genuine blessing for me as it helped me get to where I am today.

It also taught me that just because you try to shut out the 'other world' it doesn't mean things like this will stop happening to you.

5

I Just Opened My Eyes

If you are learning to trust in your soul it means you're beginning to have faith in your sixth sense. I love it when one of my hunches comes true because it makes me feel that I am fully synchronised in the moment; that I'm on track with life.

Feeling that the universe is letting you in on the bigger picture is one of the most remarkable parts of being clairvoyant. We get clairvoyant impressions regularly but more often than not we dismiss our vision or 'gut feeling' because we think we're imagining things. That is, of course, until hindsight proves otherwise and we sit back and wonder how we ever missed it in the first place.

Wouldn't it be wonderful to get a regular stream of intuitive impressions? Most of us love the idea but we feel hampered by a lack of confidence and block our clairvoyance. Perhaps you, like so many others, doubt your ability because it's hard to differentiate between a clairvoyant vision and a lively imagination? I used to get confused myself until something happened to show me how to recognise the difference.

A clairvoyant sees something that's about to happen before it actually does. Clairvoyance means clarity or 'clear sight' and this is usually expressed as symbols, pictures or events playing out like a movie in your mind. Perhaps you've experienced this sensation yourself.

On my twenty-seventh birthday I was sitting in the passenger seat of our car on the drive to work. Relaxed and contemplating where I should go for my birthday lunch, I was annoyed when a vision intruded my thoughts. The image of a blue car crashing into ours kept flashing in my head. I couldn't eliminate the vision and I remember cautioning myself, 'Stop thinking about it or you'll make it happen!'

Suddenly, the sound of screeching brakes made me jump out of my seat. I looked over my shoulder and saw a blue car swerving uncontrollably across the three-lane highway.

'Move to the right!' I urged my husband. 'He's headed straight for us!' We edged up a thin concrete median strip, narrowly avoiding oncoming traffic, and missed being hit by the blue car. Seconds later it veered into the middle lane, ploughed straight into the back of a truck and then skidded across the far left lane before hitting a brick fence. Amazingly, the driver survived. I was pretty relieved that we did too!

This incredible incident got me thinking about my vision. Did I manifest the accident because I was thinking about it or was my sixth sense warning me to take care? The next day I couldn't get visions of car accidents out of my mind but nothing eventuated. This taught me how to tell the difference between imagination and clairvoyance. While I was having visions of the blue car crashing into us an inner knowing told me it was real; the images I got on the following day didn't give me that same sense of knowing, I was just worrying.

It would be infinitely easier if a light globe went off in our head announcing when we're in psychic mode, but part of our soul-journey is to discover these subtle differences for ourselves. I don't question my sixth sense any more, I just know that it's the truth and I trust it. You can learn to do this too and make the most of your clairvoyance.

I'm always being asked, 'What's the difference between a clairvoyant and a psychic? Aren't they the same thing?' Well, yes and no. A clairvoyant is psychic but not all psychics are clairvoyant. A clairvoyant sees things in the future which means they're psychic, but not all psychics get visions or pictures of events. Some of them feel what's going on while others sense or know things without seeing visual images.

Clairvoyance isn't a logical process; it's an intuitive one. Intuition will help you make decisions but it won't give you the reason behind them. You simply get a feeling that something is right or something is wrong. If you start seeking a reason you'll end up moving into your mental state and begin intellectualising and rationalising.

Many people get stuck making a decision because they try to weigh up the pros and cons. But often this doesn't help because for every pro there is a con. Eventually they make a choice and perhaps a few weeks, or a year, later they may realise why the decision they made was right or wrong. Things don't get this complicated with clairvoyance because clairvoyance is a knowing without knowing why. It doesn't need a reason; you go with the flow. It feels right because it is right. Why? Because your ego isn't doing the talking—your soul is.

Stay open to receiving messages and accept them for what they are.

6

Whispers in My Ear

The marvellous thing about the sixth sense is that we get to experience it in our own unique way. Receiving visual intuitive messages is one of the many ways you can work with it. But some people see the future, some feel what's about to happen and others experience clairaudience, the sixth-sense ability to hear the voice of Spirit.

When I think about clairaudience I'm reminded of a truly inspiring story of an incident that happened a few years ago when a young boy fell from a ten-metre-high cliff. When the rescuers came to his aid, they were very surprised to find him alive, and even more surprised to see that he hadn't sustained any major injuries. The boy told the rescuers that as he was falling he heard a voice calling out to him, telling him to relax, and that he would be fine. As he was falling, he kept listening to this voice talking to him, keeping him relaxed. When his body hit the ground he didn't sustain the injuries one would expect from such a fall because his body wasn't tense. Just as the voice had promised him, everything was fine.

Little miracles like this happen daily but how often do we stop and think about where the voice came from? Very few people realise their miracle is the result of them listening to information that's streaming straight from Spirit. If only they could realise how truly gifted they are.

I firmly believe there's a time and place for everything and Spirit is keenly aware of this because it understands karma. Spirit steps in and speaks to us when the time is right. It comes as no surprise when I hear stories such as the one about a woman who'd never played lotto in her life, but when she walked past a newsagency heard a voice telling her to play and, following the advice, ended up winning millions. Working with our Spirit guides is delightfully serendipitous.

Clairaudience isn't always an external voice telling us what to do. Sometimes Spirit sends messages directly into our head and we hear its voice in our mind the same way we might hear songs in our head after they've been played on the radio. This happens when our guidance talks directly to our mind through what I call the 'cosmic telephone'. There's a subtle difference in the tone to the external voice. When you recognise the difference you'll be able to tell that it is coming from outside of you but being expressed within you.

Have you ever felt an odd humming or ringing in your ears that's so distracting it makes you momentarily stop what you're doing? If you have, then you've just experienced another form of clairaudience. Whenever I get this sensation I know it is my guides' way of making me sit up and pay attention, so I stop whatever it is that I'm doing and tune in to Spirit. I find this especially beneficial when my head is too full of thoughts for my guides to get through to me clairvoyantly.

If you listen carefully, sometimes you'll hear the voice of a lost soul reaching out to you asking for help. I get these requests from time to time. Recently the sound of someone knocking on my bedroom door woke me up and I heard a young girl calling out, 'Mummy, Mummy, let me in.' I got up thinking it was my teenage daughter, Chiara, but when I checked in on her, she was fast asleep.

The moment my head hit the pillow the knocking started all over again, and the voice repeated her plea, 'Mummy, Mummy, let me in.' I got up to look for her and found the lost soul of a little girl standing in the hallway looking very bewildered. This little one needed my help and I gladly crossed her over to the light, where she was reunited with the mother she was calling for. The next time you hear a voice that seems to come out of nowhere, listen carefully. It could well be the voice of someone very dear to you reaching out and keeping the bond of love going across two worlds.

Don't worry if you've never heard a guiding voice from outside or within you, it doesn't mean you're not clairaudient. Spirit is patiently awaiting your call. Why not meet them halfway by allocating some special time with them? Just nominate a certain time of the day when you can spend five minutes tuning in and listening to what Spirit has to say. I'll guarantee that in no time at all you'll feel a connection and you won't end up missing out on their valuable advice.

7

It's What I Feel

Maybe having an open telephone line to Spirit isn't your thing? That's okay because we're all different. Perhaps you're better at feeling or sensing things?

There are times when we get a special feeling about a place or person that leaves a strong impression with us. Mary, a friend of mine, told me of an experience she had when she first visited her friend Amy. While Amy went off to make coffee, Mary sat down on the comfortable lounge where she noticed a large photo of an older woman on top of the side table.

'I know it sounds crazy,' she explained. 'But as soon as I saw that photo I could smell gardenias. It lingered in the air but there were no fresh flowers in the room, no oil burners or incense and the windows were closed. But, I could smell gardenias!'

That wasn't all Mary sensed. 'I thought I was imagining things but I really did feel as though Amy's grandmother's soul was in the room, sitting next to me on the lounge.' Mary shrugged off the experience thinking it was her imagination.

Amy returned with two mugs of coffee but after a few minutes of idle chatting Mary felt compelled to ask, 'Are you burning any gardenia oil?'

Amy shook her head.

'That's strange,' said Mary. 'I can smell gardenias.'

'I don't smell anything,' replied Amy.

'Are you sure?' Mary couldn't get the gardenias off her mind. The perfume was wafting over to her from where she believed Amy's grandmother to be sitting. Something inside Mary pushed her to ask, 'Did your grandmother like gardenias?'

'She loved them!' Amy exclaimed.

Mary realised that she wasn't imagining things. Amy's grandmother really was in the room watching over her favourite grandchild.

By tuning into Amy's grandmother, Mary was having a moment of clairsentience—the ability to empathise with your surroundings. It can be expressed in a number of different ways but a very common way of experiencing clairsentience (deep feeling) is through smell. A lot of people pick up the smell of a perfume, alcohol, cigarettes or even food around the soul of departed loved ones. You could say it's their calling card. They conjure up a smell that you'd associate with them, like Amy's nan did.

Other people feel an emotion or a pain that belongs to the person standing next to them. In connecting with people our energy field fuses momentarily with the other person's; this exchange gives us the intuitive power needed to tap into their thoughts and feelings, and even the pain they're experiencing. It can be that intimate.

I can't tell you how many times I've heard someone say they haven't got a psychic bone in their body and in the same sentence tell me that their mother called that morning and before she'd even uttered a word they'd picked up on her headache! Or how they didn't know what made them walk over to a co-worker and offer assistance. They just felt the need to help them and were genuinely surprised when the co-worker opened up and admitted how overwhelmed they'd been feeling but they didn't feel comfortable asking for help.

I find it very interesting that even though our sixth sense is usually working underneath the radar of the conscious mind, we still react to the impressions we're picking up. Just because our head doesn't realise things doesn't mean our feeling-self isn't reacting.

The fantastic thing about clairsentience is being able to sense what's going on around you. It is beautiful to connect with another person and share their feelings, their hopes and joy—the uplifting affect on your heart is priceless. The not-so-fantastic thing about clairsentience is taking on board what's not yours. There are occasions when we pick up on someone else's fear, confusion or pain, which isn't so uplifting.

Unpleasant as it may be to feel someone else's headache or nausea, or their uncertainty and troubled thoughts, I believe it's still an invaluable experience because it helps you gain a deeper understanding of the fragility of the human soul. The one thing you need to remember to do is to not hold on to others' energy for too long.

I am clairsentient and it helps me gain a true insight into my clients. I've learned to disregard what my eyes show me—a sad person can always fake a smile but energy never lies. But it can be detrimental to my well being to hold on to others' thoughts and feelings for any length of time. Once I've got the insight I need I cut the cord that connects me to my client and release all the energy that doesn't belong to me. I do this by visualising a white light cutting and dissolving the cord between us. Once the link is broken I'm no longer absorbing disruptive emotions and I immediately feel lighter and brighter and can get on with my job.

If you are clairsentient it can help you in all kinds of ways, for example it can give you a true feel for what's happening with family and work. Just remember that you can have the empathy you need to be of service to others without the complications of holding on to their energies simply by knowing when to disconnect.

8

Reaching for the Other Side

The most satisfying experiences in life come from feelings of relatedness—a sense of closeness to others and a connection to all things. That's why losing someone you love can be crippling. One minute they're here, a very real part of your life; a moment later they're gone, lost forever in the blanket of death, beyond reach. I know death can leave a lingering emptiness inside, that it can be hard to accept. The pain of loss chips away at your heart because you can't touch your loved one any more. When they were alive you could feel them, hug them and share your hopes and wishes with them. You could check in on them and see how things were going. But the veil of death hides its secrets from most.

But, what if there was a way to reach them? The sixth-sense gift of mediumship bridges the gap between life and death. It helps reunite you with the people you have lost.

I was in the middle of a reading for Caroline when I saw a man standing next to her.

'I have your father here,' I said. She looked surprised.

'Dad?'

'Well, if his name is Charles, then yes, I have your dad here.'

She started laughing. 'That's incredible. Here's here in Spirit?'

'Yes. He's telling me that you were right, and something about he's the proof.'

Caroline laughed triumphantly, which surprised me. Usually people get emotional.

'That's priceless.' She grinned like the Cheshire cat.

After a few moments she explained. 'Dad was an atheist. My mum's side of the family were spiritualist—my nan was a medium. After my parents divorced Dad took me out of the country to live in South Africa. Over the years I lost contact with Mum's side of the family. Dad would never let me talk about spiritual stuff and he insisted there was no such thing as life after death.'

'Well, he's changed his tune,' I said. 'He's telling me, "You win.".'

Caroline was thrilled. 'A few years ago I flew home to be by his bedside. A day before he died of cancer I asked him if he still believed there was no life after death. He made a bet with me. If there was life after death he'd eat humble pie. He promised to visit me and tell me he was wrong!' A tear rolled down her cheek.

Mediums are spiritual messengers, go-betweens linking two worlds together. Their sixth-sense gift is being able to connect to the Spirit world and the person who has passed over. Once connected, they can tell you many things you want to know about your loved one. They can share information such as what they were like when they were alive, how they died, what they've been doing while in the Spirit world and exactly what's been happening around you. Banish any notion that the person you have lost is out of touch!

A good medium will give you concrete information to validate that your loved one is with you in Spirit. But even when they have this proof it can still take time for some people to digest the information, probably because they think its surreal to be able to connect with the dead.

On the seventh anniversary of my dad's death, I was teaching a class when I felt him hanging around me. I asked my students to tune in and tell me who it was. One student said, 'I'm getting the name Michael.' She quizzed the soul and told me, 'Is he your father?' I pressed her for more information. 'He's telling me he worked on the Snowy Mountains scheme.'

I had always had it in the back of my head that Dad worked there when he first came to Australia in the early 1950s. I went to visit Mum that night and she was cross with me.

'You didn't even go to visit his grave,' she scolded.

'Mum, you know I don't need to visit his grave to talk to him. He paid me a visit in class today.'

'You know that stuff makes me uneasy,' she said.

'I know. But he was with me. If only you could know how special it is having him speaking with my students. He told one of them that he'd worked on the Snowy Mountains Scheme when he first arrived here.'

'Your father never worked in the mountains,' she said, crossing her arms.

'Where did Dad work in 1952–53?' I asked her.

She thought for a moment. 'In Cooma.'

I laughed. 'Mum, that's where most of the men who were working on the Snowy Mountains Scheme lived.'

She shook her head. 'I can't believe you didn't visit his grave!'

A healthy dose of scepticism is a good thing. It doesn't matter how many books you've read, or stories you've heard, until a message meets your expectations it's perfectly reasonable to remain sceptical. It's not until you hear what you need to hear the way you need to hear it, that it clicks for you.

Recently I took my sisters to see a medium's public appearance because they wanted proof of life after death from someone who didn't know anything about them. The medium began by telling the audience that she had an older lady with her who was talking about her daughter who had half an arm missing. My aunt had severely injured her arm in an accident and lost half of her right arm. The medium then described our grandmother as well as things about our own mother and what had been happening in my sisters' lives.

Then she turned to me and said, 'You've been to Africa.' I shook my head. 'You're planning a trip to Africa. I'm seeing a safari, African men carrying bags. Who in the family has been to Africa?' I told her no one.

I wasn't concerned. Mediums, like other psychics, do make mistakes. We all have our good and bad days and can also misinterpret information that Spirit has given us.

The next day my sisters were telling Mum about the medium and what she had also said about Africa. Mum nodded her head. 'Your grandfather went on safari for a few weeks before he had to go into active duty during World War Two.' So there was a link with Africa after all.

Mediums do a fantastic job in helping us deal with death. Their messages heal people, helping many to gain closure and overcome their fear of death.

Talking with your loved ones

Anyone can talk to their loved ones in Spirit. Here's what you need to do:

Start by asking for a loved one in Spirit to visit you. Set aside a time when you know no one is going to disturb you and begin by asking your guardian angel or your Spirit guides to seal your house in a lovely golden light to energetically protect it. This means that nothing can get into your house unless you give it permission to enter. When you are ready, close your eyes and ask one family member to come in (you don't want a whole bunch, it will get too confusing). Ask them to stand about a metre in front of you. Hold out your arm with your palm upwards and feel the energy in front of you. Does it feel familiar? Is there a fragrance like their favourite perfume or aftershave? Keep your eyes closed and visualise them in your mind. Now, let them talk to you.

9

The Thing About Energy

Spirits have individual vibes, just like we do. Mediums develop their ability to sense different vibes around them. It helps them read energy so they can pass on messages from Spirit. You can do this too once you understand the basics of energy.

Energy is the driving force behind all of creation. It's everywhere. The way energy is expressed makes a huge difference to how we relate or react to it. But how often do you think about it? Surprisingly, most of us rarely think about the unseen energy that holds the universe together.

Once, when she was fifteen, my daughter Chiara was yelling and jumping up and down on her bed when I came running in. 'Mum, Mum, the backpack on the floor is moving by itself!' She was half laughing, half scared. 'Look! Can you see it moving? Get the ghost out of here!'

'Oh, is that all? I thought it was a ferocious mouse.'

'Not funny, Mum!'

I explained her guides were moving the bag in order to grab her attention.

'Close your eyes, Chiara, and feel the energy of the room. What does it feel like?'

A minute later she opened her eyes. 'Okay, yeah, it feels good. So, nice guides huh?'

When you feel unfamiliar vibes, stop and take a nice deep breath in and try to relax. It's easier to assess a situation when you're not reacting to it, so let go of your fear. Now close your eyes and tune in and feel the energy of your surroundings. How does it make you feel? Energy doesn't lie: if it feels good, then it is. If family or Spirit guides are hanging around you'll feel a lighter and higher vibration because they have an unmistakable divine energy. You won't feel negative vibes around them.

Energy isn't just outside you. Every time you laugh, cry or feel love, your feelings create emotions. And you feel that energy, don't you? Laughing makes every cell in your body light up, while sadness drags you down—it's powerful. Emotional energy is strong enough that you can even feel other people's emotions. A hug is just a hug, but a hug infused with love is electrifying.

Everything, every person, every thought, every action, every feeling is energy. And energy can't be destroyed; it can be changed, but it can't be destroyed. Water can be liquid, ice or a gas; the only thing that really changes is how fast or slow the molecules are moving—in other words, the vibration of its energy. What does this tell us about life? That nothing really dies; it just changes its vibration from one energetic form to another.

You can use this simple principle to change negative vibes in or around you into positive ones. Don't ever forget that our thoughts and feelings are energy and that they're a lot more powerful than we realise. If you're consistently thinking negative thoughts then you're creating negative energies; if you're thinking positive thoughts then you're creating positive vibes around you. These thoughts and feelings affect your inner chemistry and your aura, so they're affecting every aspect of you—your wellbeing, relationships, work, finances and dreams.

I'm fascinated by Dr Masaru Emoto's research into how projected thoughts and feelings affect water crystals. He found that sending thoughts of love to water created beautiful symmetrical shaped crystals while lower-vibe emotions like hate created polluted or deformed crystals. Since our physical bodies are made up of about sixty per cent water, this should surely make us think about the effects of our own thoughts and feelings.

Have a think about the impact energy has on your life. How are your thoughts and feelings affecting your wellbeing? How does your vibe affect your family and friends? How are you working your energies?

10

Reading the Signs

We often respond spontaneously to energy. Even if you think, 'I can't feel energy,' it doesn't mean you're not responding or reacting to it. Have you ever noticed how your boss's mood affects everyone else in the office? Or, when a friend tells you 'everything's great' but your heart automatically prompts you to say, 'Hey, what's wrong?'

Responding to energy is one thing. But imagine being able to read it. Wouldn't that give you a lovely edge on things? The sixth sense helps you do this by collecting information from other people's energy. It gives you a feel for what's really going on. I've always found that when I use the sixth sense to energetically read situations I end up making better life choices.

When my daughter Chiara was three years old the doctor diagnosed her with a urinary tract infection (UTI). He cautioned me to keep an eye on her and to take her to hospital if her condition deteriorated. It deteriorated quickly. Her temperature skyrocketed and she was listless. The emergency ward intern told us, 'It's only a UTI. We'll give you some antibiotics and then she can go home.'

My sixth sense told me the intern was wrong. I read Chiara's energy and I immediately knew we had a real crisis on our hands. If you're a parent you'll know what I'm talking about. The sixth sense link between a parent and their child is incredible. It's an in-built monitor that can tell you things like what baby really wants when they're crying or, if you're outside in the garden, you can suddenly sense that you need to go back inside because baby is waking up.

I pressed the doctor to review his diagnosis but he insisted Chiara be released. I spent ten minutes debating the issue but ultimately he ignored my pleas and was signing off Chiara's case notes when she started convulsing. The doctor had thought I was being an overreactive mother, not the intuitive I am. As it turned out, Chiara's blood was thickening from dehydration, bacteria had crossed from the kidneys into her blood and she had septicaemia, which can kill within twenty-four hours!

That night Chiara's temperature climbed to 41.2 degrees. I used my sixth sense to ask my guides to show me the future. Would Chiara survive? Then I got a clairvoyant image of Chiara as an adult. She was going to be ok! In this sort of stressful situation it is not uncommon for mothers to get very little sleep but I trusted my sixth sense and I slept like a baby. I read the situation correctly and made the right choice. It's during moments like this that I am so glad I rely on my sixth sense.

Once you start recognising that your thoughts and feelings translate into energy, you'll understand how it's possible to intuitively read people and situations, as well as peer into the future.

Although we're always responding to different energies on a daily basis, we're usually unaware of the effects these energies are having on us. However, if you make a subtle adjustment by switching on your sixth sense, you'll be astounded by what you find. You will see that you're being showered with the most beautiful cosmic energies imaginable—invisible, intelligent universal energy.

The easiest way to describe universal energy is to say that it's the basic driving force behind all creation. This energy doesn't just surround us, it permeates through us, and so we feel it at every level of our being.

Nothing can exist without energy. The most wonderful aspect of universal energy is that it's imbued with cosmic consciousness—it's intelligent and eternal. It's the energy that creates stardust. Both you and I and this wonderful world are made from the same stardust. Without it we wouldn't exist.

11

Activating Your Sixth Sense

Every day a stream of universal energy enters us. It comes through the transpersonal point, an energy centre located about thirty to sixty centimetres above your head that passes through the chakras which use this energy to nourish the body and soul. A chakra is a spinning vortex of energy that governs a particular aspect of consciousness. They act as individual, yet interrelated, centres that connect the mind, body and Spirit. One of your chakras is the third eye, which is the seat of your consciousness, your perception and visions. Chakras are important for your development because they help activate your sixth sense. To maximise your sixth-sense gift I recommend finetuning your chakras because having completely balanced chakras gives you the perfect mind, body and soul connection. This heightens your personal vibration, which makes it so much easier to access and work with the sixth sense.

The transpersonal point is a centre that your soul uses to regulate exactly how much information is allowed to come into your mind at any one time. Practices such as meditation will expand your transpersonal point which will in turn enhance your ability to connect with Spirit. Trust me on this one; you will get a fantastic flood of information from Spirit when your transpersonal point is wide open.

When you start working with your sixth sense your transpersonal point and your third eye begin to stretch. As they stretch, they allow increasing amounts of information and inspiration from Spirit to filter through to your awareness. In turn, this strengthens your sixth sense and broadens your outlook on life. Don't be daunted by the prospect of working with this energy. It's a perfectly natural energy and you've been unconsciously reacting to it all your life.

Mark's transpersonal point was open, helping him to use his sixth sense, but he didn't realise it.

'I used to help the kids with their school work and I was amazed at how little they knew. I would ask them, "Didn't you go through this with your teacher?"

'"The teacher? Oh, she was more worried that Ben was throwing paper, that Lauren was yelling, and Josh and Kim were spit-balling all over the room."

'And more than once I thought, "Geez, I should become a teacher. I know I could do better than many of them."

'But it was only a passing thought. I had several degrees and other credentials behind me ranging from engineering and science to naturopathy. You name it, I did it. When I started practising naturopathy, my clients would say, "Hey, Mark, I love the way you simplify things. I can understand it when you say it that way. You'd make a great teacher." Then I saw Sue for a reading, and she said, "Mark, I see you teaching. You're a natural."

'My response was, "Yeah, I've thought about it," but that was as far as it went. It wasn't until my business took a hit during the economic downturn that I felt that maybe what my intuition had been telling me, and what Sue told me, was right. I finally decided to look at it.

'Now, I'm at the end of my education degree and I'm out doing prac teaching. The feedback I get from the kids at school is, "Sir, you have a great way of explaining things." One kid said to another teacher, "You know that new teacher, Mark? Geez, sir, he knows a lot."'

Mark's sixth sense knew this all along.

12

Trust Your Sixth Sense Regardless

It's never too late to start working with your sixth sense. I'm going to show you how to harness the energy from your transpersonal point so you can work it to your advantage. This exercise will help you connect with the universal energy. It will help you open your psychic eye and expand your perception.

> Close your eyes and relax. Visualise a lovely white light streaming into your transpersonal point. Take your awareness there and feel this energy. Ask that it helps you to expand your consciousness. Then let the energy stream into your head. Take your awareness to the centre of your forehead and visualise this white light slowly opening your third eye.

Now say, 'I wish to activate my psychic abilities,' and then flush the third-eye chakra with a luminous indigo light until you feel this chakra expanding.

Sherry has been learning how to expand her transpersonal point after a twenty-year self-imposed block on using her gift.

'When I was a teenager I used to be able to put my hands on someone and be able to "see" injuries inside of them but I blocked off this ability after it ended in frustration for me.

'I was at a football match and one of my boyfriend's friends was injured. The coach was treating it with a heat pack, however when I touched the injured boy, I saw that a tendon had been torn deep inside the joint where the hip connects to the leg and that the heat was aggravating the tear. He needed ice and to go to hospital. The coach got very annoyed at me and told me to get lost when I suggested that perhaps a heat pack wasn't the best option, so I just whispered to the guy the name of the tendon that was torn and told him to tell them that when he got to the hospital. Turns out I was right, including the name of the damaged tendon, but I didn't like to do it any more because it scared me. I didn't understand. Now there's no holding me back.'

Cathy needed a helping hand to boost her confidence. I taught her how to open her transpersonal point and connect with her higher self. After we did this I felt she was ready to put her ability to the test at one of my psychic live performance events. She stood up in front of a room of people and she was absolutely surprised how much information came through.

Afterwards, she came over to me and said, 'Sue, wow, it turned out to be so clear and accurate. I can't believe I had a bunch of total strangers sitting in the audience validating what my sixth sense was telling me! It made me realise how powerful this information is and that it should be communicated carefully and with respect.'

Perhaps you, or someone you know, have had a sixth sense feeling but people laughed, or gave you negative feedback. It can be enough to discourage you. If you rise above criticism, and follow what your heart is telling you, you'll always be right.

13

How to See and Feel Energy

Before you build a new house you employ an architect to draw up plans so the builders know where things have to go. Well, your soul has a lovely whitish-blue energy that contains a blueprint that tells your body what to do. Everything that happens at a soul-level works its way into the etheric body and eventually plays out in your physical body. The etheric body is the part of the aura that acts like a blueprint for the body. If you are in tune with your soul, the etheric body can be maintained in peak condition which helps your wellbeing. Try these exercises to activate your ability to see and feel energy:

How to see energy

Ask a friend to stand by a plain coloured wall. Let your eyes go out of focus and tune in until you start to see a whitish-blue (or pale blue) glow emanating about one inch (2.5 centimetres) from their body. This is the energy of their etheric body.

How to feel energy

Focus your attention further away from your friend's body and tune in. See if you can see any colours or movement of energy.

Ask your friend to stand in front of you. Ask Spirit that you attune to feeling energy through your hands, then visualise white light opening the sensitivity in your hands. Slowly run your left hand down alongside their body (about one inch, or 2.5 centimetres away from it). Tune in. You may feel a slight tingling or a gentle pressure pushing your hand away. Now try running your hand alongside their arm, this time with your eyes closed. Feel their vibration. As you do this you are using your long forgotten sense, your sixth sense.

14

How to Live the High Life

Once you've opened the gateway to the Spirit world through your transpersonal point you can get down to business and develop your sixth sense. Your sixth sense is a lot like a piece of rough rock, just waiting to be smoothed so it can shine like river pebbles. Once you've polished up your sixth sense and have it shining, there's nothing holding you back from working with your intuition on all levels.

If you would love to work with your sixth sense but don't know where to start, I know how you feel. I thought it was going to be complicated and demanding too, but, much to my surprise, it was a lot easier than I expected once I let go of a few unrealistic expectations.

My biggest stumbling block was the belief that I was never allowed to make a mistake. Remember Rhondda, the lady who cleared the lost soul from my home? She became my teacher. On my first day in class, just before we started to meditate, she turned to me and said, 'I want you to draw the Spirit guide you see in this meditation.'

I laughed at the ridiculous request. As if I was going to see a Spirit guide! She handed me a pencil and some paper and said, 'Trust that you will see a guide. I know you can already draw.'

During the meditation I met a man who said he was Rhondda's father and that he was here keeping an eye on her one-year-old daughter, Catherine, who was asleep upstairs. I'd no idea about this. The class was held at Rhondda's house, so it was feasible. I asked him why he was watching Rhondda's daughter.

'Because Catherine has a cold and I like to visit her when she's not well.'

After I finished my drawing, Rhondda asked me who I saw. I laughed, 'A Spirit that said he was your dad. Really, it's only my imagination!'

'Is it?' She smiled as she took the drawing from me. 'Ok, guys,' she said. 'I want everyone to step into the dining room.'

She opened the door and we all trundled into the room. On the china cabinet there was a photo. Rhondda held it up with her left hand. 'This is Dad.' Then she raised my picture in her right hand. 'And this is Dad!'

I did get it right. But after that day I was not able to do another guide drawing for over a year. Why? Because I didn't believe I could repeat my brilliant one-off performance. What I was really saying to myself was, 'I don't have confidence in me.'

Other people experience problems opening up their sixth sense because of impatience. They want to be amazing right away. Honestly, there's no point rushing things; you'll only end up putting yourself under too much pressure. Nothing is ever achieved under the burden of unrealistic expectations.

Let your sixth sense unfold gradually. Real progress is achieved one step at a time.

So, where to start?

The best way to unlock your gifts is to get in touch with your inner self. Getting to know 'you' is important. Through self-awareness you'll discover which restrictive beliefs or patterns are holding you back from working with your sixth sense. This part requires a little elbow grease to help tackle the grimy bits, all those limiting beliefs and issues you carry around with you.

Restrictive thoughts and feelings, and unresolved fears, form the basis for what we call energy blocks. These blocks lower your personal vibration, so it makes sense to clear them. Meditating or working through the chakras helps you uncover these limiting aspects of yourself that hold you back.

So let's start by creating a little quiet time to do some inner house cleaning for the soul. Use this opportunity to address any negative thoughts or fears you have about developing your abilities.

Here's what you can do:

Close your eyes and visualise a white light coursing through your body. Ask that it stops in the area of your body where you sense that there's an energy block. Take your awareness within and follow the light until you reach an organ, or organs, where the energy is trapped.

Now feel the underlying emotion. Is it fear, anger, hurt, resentment, frustration? Let the emotion surface and see if you can get a visual image of a time or place in your life when this issue was being laid down. Relax and let images pop into your mind's eye—images from your past that hold the key to the origin of the feeling. Once you've discovered the emotion and the cause of the block, you will have the perfect starting point to heal and dissolve it.

Emma discovered that the true origin of her repressed anger came from a disempowering workplace situation. Talk about stretching yourself too far to please others! After Emma put everyone else's work ahead of her own, her boss was on her case. Her own work was falling behind and she was making too many mistakes. Everyone expected 'Ms Fix It' to help but no one was offering to help Emma now that she needed it. I pointed out to Emma that passive-aggressive people suppress their real anger. Doing the above exercise highlighted how much of the emotion her body was really storing.

When I tried doing this exercise for the first time, I didn't get too much from it. It's funny how I resisted change. But I kept going and it became easier. So don't give up if you hit an inner brick wall. Eventually you'll break through and tackle restrictive thoughts and feelings.

Once you start clearing restrictive energies, your vibration naturally starts rising, and this is an essential ingredient in activating the sixth sense.

Relax. Close your eyes and visualise a lovely column of orange light washing through to the organ or part of the body where the energy block is. Focus on the emotional wound that you'd like to release. Acknowledge the wound, and give yourself permission to release it. Visualise a lovely healing bubble of blue and pink light forming in your sacral chakra. Ask that it slowly releases healing energy over the next twenty-four hours.

15

Creating a Little Magic in Your Life

Changing energy is the secret behind magic. Not the type of elaborate illusions magicians perform, but real magic. Real people create real magic all the time and I'm a firm believer in its power. The way to create a little magic in your life is through manifestation.

So, how do you create something out of nothing? You don't have to be an alchemist. All you need is to understand how the energy of manifestation works on subtle levels and the concept that whatever is inside us is reflected on the outside.

The first step in manifesting is to become aware of the direction of your thoughts and feelings. If you keep attracting the wrong people or the wrong situations you need to take a good look at what type of vibes you're giving out to the world. Are you holding on to lots of negative thoughts, tension, stress or feelings of inadequacy in your energy system? If you are, guess what you are drawing back. Have you ever noticed that when you are feeling good, when you are positive and optimistic, things tend to fall into place and that feel-good factor keeps coming back?

You manifest through visualisation—see it play out in your mind first, and then visualise yourself receiving it as though it has already happened. If disruptive thoughts like, 'This is never going to happen,' or, 'I don't deserve this,' creep into your mind, let them go. Re-focus and concentrate on your positive visualisation until it's completed. Now, give your visualisation permission to happen. Allow the energy behind your intention, your visualisation, to take form in the ethers. This will act like a scaffolding system that will attract the right energy to build your dream.

How well manifestation works depends on the energy behind it. We create what we believe. If you believe in something strongly enough, and you direct that energy, time and time again, eventually you have a very real chance of manifesting it.

But as the saying goes, be careful what you wish for. Robert discovered this the hard way.

I had asked my parapsychology students to manifest something their soul desired. Robert shot up his hand and asked, 'Can I ask for a million dollars?'

I said, 'Is that what your soul really wants?'

'Of course,' he replied enthusiastically.

'Just check with your higher self,' I cautioned.

After the guided manifestation meditation Robert opened his eyes and smirked. I shot him a look.

'I couldn't help myself,' he said.

A week later Robert turned up to class looking disheartened. Some students laughed, 'What Robert, no millions?'

Robert furrowed his brow, 'Sue,' he said, 'You're not going to believe this but the day after doing the manifestation meditation I went to withdraw some money and there was $999,999.99 in my account. It was unbelievable; there should have been $200 in it. I did it! A few days later I got a call from the bank saying, "Robert, we need to talk".'

Robert couldn't understand how he could manifest the million dollars only to lose it less than a week later. I explained that he got what he asked for, but there was never any guarantee he could *keep* what he asked for. This is why you need to be careful *how* you ask for things. Also, there are times you might get what you want but it may come at a cost. You might gain this one thing, but lose something else.

It is also important to remember to allow your intentions to manifest in their own time. Sometimes we're so keen to get things happening that we become attached to the outcome, whether it's the right timing for our higher good or not. If you energetically hold on to what you want, it will block the natural flow of your creative energies. With a little patience and grace things will manifest when they need to manifest.

Have you been able to manifest things successfully? Perhaps you know someone who is constantly being blocked? Remember that the key to manifesting is to correctly and consistently project positive thoughts out to the ethers. Eventually it will happen for you. By using your sixth sense (for example, using clairvoyance to get a vision, clairaudience to hear messages or clairsentience to feel what's right) you'll get in touch with what your soul wants. You'll be guided to make choices that are right for you, choices that align with what your soul needs to manifest instead of what your ego wants.

When you manifest from the heart, when you're in touch with what your soul knows is what you need, then the heavens will open up and shower you with gifts. It may take a little longer, but what you get will be so much more rewarding and satisfying.

16

Be Careful What You Wish For

If you are going to create a little practical magic take a few moments to consider how getting what you wish for is going to affect you. Sometimes we want something so much we forget to think about the consequences that come with it.

You must understand that whatever you want to manifest cannot be done in a moment—you can't just put a thought out there and expect it to happen overnight. You have to live it and consistently believe it, as if it has already happened. And you have to understand how personal karma works.

Karma is the law of cause and effect. This means that everything you do has consequences—you're either creating new karma, or clearing out old karma through your thoughts, feelings and actions. I like to call karma the equaliser because it is energy trying to find balance. If the scales are lopsided it means you still have karma to deal with, which means having to make adjustments in your thinking, feeling and actions in order to achieve a balance in your karmic energy. Sometimes, you are the one creating new karma; at other times you may be balancing karma from your past-life deeds. Some people have their own karma to work through with you. Why not tune in and let your sixth sense tell you what your own karma is and how to resolve it?

One day I was walking through a shopping centre with my young niece, Simone, when she saw a twenty-dollar note on the floor. She ran over and picked it up.

'Aunty Sue, can I spend it?' she asked brightly.

I smiled and was about to say yes when I noticed an elderly man who was slowly making his way towards the exit. The lining of his trouser pocket was hanging out. I knew the money had to be his, and my sixth sense confirmed it. Simone and I ran up to him and handed him the money, and the smile on his face said it all.

Initially Simone was a little miffed because she didn't get to keep the money. I explained to her that he was a pensioner and that the money was important to him.

'Doesn't it make you feel good that you made him smile?'

'Yes,' she smiled feeling very proud of herself.

The next day Simone and I were back in the same shopping centre. We were at a checkout when I realised I didn't have my handbag. I used my sixth sense to locate where I left it and got a vision of the bench in the middle of the mall where we'd sat earlier. Since I'd left it in a public place I held little hope of finding it. But as I approached the bench I saw a lovely older lady sitting next to my handbag.

She looked up and smiled. 'I thought you would come back so I waited for you.'

Not all karma happens as quickly or obviously as that, but karma will always bring an energy of equal value back to you. Our random act of kindness was returned with another random act of kindness.

Karma shapes your life lessons, the experiences the soul needs to learn. It helps you make sense of events—why certain things happen, how one thing leads to another—it's a lovely intricate web. Getting in touch with your karma helps you on your journey through life. What you're doing today determines what energies come your way in the future.

When you align your hopes and wishes to what your soul wants, you'll find it's so much easier to create magical moments. If you're trying to manifest something that's not on your karmic path it may take longer to manifest, or it may never manifest at all. This is why getting in touch with your personal karma is important.

17

Unleash Your Past

Have you ever thought about the kind of karma you had in a past life? Some of this karma is playing out for you right now.

When working with your sixth sense don't be surprised if you occasionally get flashbacks from another time and place. At first you might be a little confused because these images are foreign to you. That's because these are visions from the places you've visited and people you've known during one of your many past lives.

Delving into your past lives can be a very rewarding process that really helps you to understand who you are now. Using your sixth sense, you can also tap into the past lives of family and friends and help them gain some valuable insights into their own soul-history. Being psychic means you are able to transverse time and space, so connecting with the past is as easy as peering into the future.

While eastern cultures embraced reincarnation thousands of years ago, here in the west it has only been in recent years that we've seen a lovely explosion in the awareness of past lives. This is largely because of the new age movement and research by people like Dr Brian Weiss who wrote the groundbreaking book, *Many Lives, Many Masters*.

Dr Weiss, the head of a psychiatric department in a major hospital, started exploring the idea of past lives after a hypnosis session with a troubled client, Catherine, opened a door to a new way of looking at reality. Dr Weiss discovered that most of Catherine's fears were intimately connected with past life memories. Catherine feared choking, water, aeroplanes and the dark, and she was terrified of dying. While in a hypnotic trance Catherine was able to recall past life memories which proved to be the foundation of her present-day problems. And once she'd had this fantastic insight many of her fears and phobias disappeared.

When the fourteenth Dalai Lama was discovered in 1937 by a lama and a government official disguised as merchants, he was two-and-a-half years old. The disguised lama, Kewstang Rinpoche, using his sixth sense, had a clear vision of where the boy was to be found—a village with a three-storied monastery with a gold and jade roof. The boy's house would have turquoise tiles and a brown and white spotted dog in the courtyard.

The boy claimed that the beads Kewstang Rinpoche was wearing were his own. The lama told the boy that he could have the beads if he could guess who he was talking to. The boy replied in the dialect of central Tibet, a dialect unknown in his district, and told the merchant that he was a lama of Sera.

The lama returned some time later with certain articles that had belonged to the thirteenth Dalai Lama including his spectacles, silver pencil and eating bowl. He also had some articles which were duplicates to test the boy—a black rosary, a yellow rosary, two walking sticks and a small ivory hand drum used in religious devotions. The boy, Lhamo Thondup, correctly identified each item that had belonged to the thirteenth Dalai Lama.

This is how powerful past-life memories can be. Why not use your sixth sense to unleash your past? Your soul is rich in memories of the incredible sights and sounds of places that no longer physically exist, but are still alive and well in your cellular memory. While you may explore these lives for curiosity's sake, know that the sensory information you gather will help you understand what lies beneath some of your deep fears and phobias, which in turn will help you to clear them. You can also discover your soul-links with others and how you can enrich your relationships.

Penny asked me to uncover one of her past lives. I tuned in and saw her as a twenty-six-year-old woman living in Italy during the Renaissance. She was giving birth to her third child, a baby boy, but she knew she would die during the birth and was feeling guilty because she wouldn't be present in his life.

I said, 'Penny, I'm getting age twenty-six. Were you pregnant with your third child when you were twenty-six?'

'Yes, why?' she said, the question surprising her. I then explained all the images I was receiving.

'Did you have a medical emergency before or during the birth?' I asked.

She nodded. 'I nearly lost Steven before he was born.'

'You may have tried to compensate for that past life. Do you feel you wrapped him up in cotton wool?'

'Yes, I've always felt like I needed to go out of my way for him because he nearly died.'

I explained the deep connection between her and her son's souls, which stemmed from their lifetime in Renaissance Italy. This time she was definitely going to be around to raise him. It's interesting that he was the one who nearly left this time around. I felt it balanced things out. How beautiful that they can be mother and son properly this time.

•

Do you want to find out more about your own past lives? Here's a simple past-life focus you can do to find out who you have been previously and how that experience is affecting you today.

Relax and go into a meditation and visualise being in a library. Feel yourself being drawn to a particular book. When you open the book you will see a picture of a place. Feel this image drawing you in and let it take you back to the time and place in history it depicts. See yourself stepping into the town, village or landscape you lived in, look at the architecture, at your surrounds, and let your senses drink in the atmosphere of the place. Look down at your feet. Are they the feet of a man, woman or child? What kind of clothes are you wearing? Spend some time exploring your old home and the person you were back then.

Tuning in to our past lives gives us the opportunity to put old issues to bed and reminds us of the strong karmic links between us and the special people in our lives. Better still, you'll definitely get to see what mistakes not to repeat this time around.

18

I Know You

One of the most intriguing parts of past-life karma is how the past-life memories can trigger wafts of deja vu when you least expect it. I'm sure you've experienced moments of deja vu, the sense of having previously experienced something even though you know you haven't. Have you ever visited a place for the very first time and been taken aback because it's so familiar? That's the feeling. It's like walking into a crowded room at a new venue and seeing someone for the very first time and feeling the strangest sensation of recognition wash over you. Intuitively you know this person, even though logically you know that you don't. You can be excused for feeling a little confounded by this situation because you can't rationalise what you're experiencing and feeling.

The feeling of deja vu surfaces when something triggers your cellular memory of a similar situation or person. It might be an experience from childhood or from a past life, or it could be derived from a dream you had a long time ago. The energy of deja vu is full of subtle nuances and the simplest things can bring it to life. You could be walking past a garden and the perfume of the roses might awaken a memory, or a feeling that you've been in that exact moment before. Your sixth sense is wired to tune into the feeling of deja vu as a way of reminding you of the interconnectivity of the past and present.

A really lovely way of looking at memory in general is to see it as a pattern of resonating energy that's stored in your cells. This energy serves as a link to the past, a thread connecting you to experiences both from this life and previous ones. This thread holds thoughts and feelings, so it's a record of your personal history. This energy stays very much alive within you despite the passage of time.

•

We were sitting in an outdoor restaurant on Syntagma Square in Athens, having called off a walk to the Acropolis because of a heatwave. It was so lovely sitting in the shade enjoying a cool drink and a light meal; the Acropolis would wait for us.

My friends were happily chatting away but my attention was suddenly hijacked by a delicious sense of deja vu. It felt so real. I was transported back to the 1920s and saw myself sitting in the very same spot. I was a man and the scent of cigars lingered in the air. The afternoon sun was bright and warm on my bronze skin. I was drinking retsina with a friend and we were engaged in a passionate debate about my landscape paintings and his sculptures.

Suddenly I was snatched back from the past and returned to the present. How bewildering! I painted landscapes but I wasn't into landscapes in my current life. I liked to paint people because I loved exploring emotions. The weird thing was that I wasn't really keen about Athens either, but had felt compelled to travel there. It was like an invisible rope had been pulling and pulling to lure me back to this spot for a reason.

Minutes later I got another flashback—the sense of deja vu was getting stronger. I looked like I was about thirty. I was standing with a palette on my arm on a pebbly beach not far from where some fishermen were sitting repairing their nets. Their boat bobbed up and down on a gentle current and a rope stretched across the vessel with their octopus catch drying in the sun.

I get another flash. I was happily walking through a graveyard near a church and somehow I knew that this church was important to me. 'Sue . . . Sue! Are you okay?' A voice broke the mesmerising spell of the past.

I stared at my friends. They had no idea where my head was at.

Six months after I returned from overseas I discovered why I had a strong hit of deja vu while in Athens. One day my teacher decided to tune in to each of us in class and give us a few insights about one of our past lives. I had never told her about my trip but when it was my turn, the first thing she said was, 'Sue, you were an artist. You lived in Athens in the early twentieth century. I see you—you're a man. You painted pictures for the local church, not saintly icon stuff, but ones of the sea and the space and the people around you.'

She then looked at Stephen, who was my boyfriend at the time. 'He was your best friend in that life. He was a sculptor and carved the headstones for the graveyard near the church. I'm being shown that you died in your early thirties because of your lifestyle.'

•

If you experience a feeling of deja vu you should stop what you're doing and spend a few moments tuning into it. Don't try to rationalise the experience, just feel it and let the subtle atmosphere of the space take over. Feel it, explore it, live it. You can always analyse it later on. People tend to get stuck during a moment of deja vu because they're busy trying to work out what's really going on, trying to piece the feeling and their experience together. You need to recognise the energy of the situation and realise you are experiencing exactly the same energy from a previous moment in time and that is why you're getting that tantalising feeling of deja vu.

Deja vu gives you little clues to help you link a part of your current life to where you've already been and to where you need to be going. It could be asking you to respond or act differently, or it could help you make the connection to someone you knew in a previous life. Sometimes you'll simply recognise an energetic 'familiarity' and other times it may relate to something you've experienced during a dream a long time ago and completely forgotten. It shows how our reality operates on so many different levels.

There is something alluring about deja vu. These moments fill us with the most incredible sensations; they are captivating, timeless moments that connect two different times and places. Deja vu can help you remember a part of who you once were, or help you understand irrational fears and phobias, or why you're drawn to certain people. It reminds us that life is full of surprising richness and shows us the true depth of our sensory potential. Isn't it fantastic to have your sixth sense working like this?

19

A Sneak Peek

The captivating, timeless moment when deja vu floods your senses is unforgettable. Who can ignore its rich, lingering aroma? But there's another sixth-sense gift that fascinates us, an adventure which some people are fortunate enough to have. If you ever have a near-death experience, you'll never forget it.

You're drifting up a tunnel of light. At the end of the tunnel some luminous beings are coming to lovingly greet you. Among them you may recognise loved ones who have already passed over. 'I don't think we're in Kansas any more, Toto,' you say to yourself. You know you should be scared, but somehow you're not. The luminous beings are smiling at you, and you feel the warmth and radiance of their smiles. One of them reaches out and holds your hand. Where are you? You're in the timeless place between life and death.

A near-death experience isn't final; it's just a taste of what's waiting around the corner. Most people who have a near-death experience are greatly affected by it once they awake. People find it easier to feel love and compassion and many find a new life direction. They now know that life goes on beyond this one and they are freed from the fear of death. What a wonderful feeling, to be liberated from a fear that lies buried deep within most of us.

Fred was happy to sit up in his hospital bed and tell his family about his amazing experience.

'I was walking down a white hallway with two closed doors. Marie-Grace [a family friend in Spirit] came up to me and told me that if I opened one door I could go with her. If I opened the other door I'd get to come back here for a short while. Then she said, "You can't open the first door right now. You're not ready yet. But you will be in a few months time."'

'It's just a dream,' said his wife Tina, not wanting to think about his death.

He smiled tenderly at his wife of over fifty years. 'I'm alright. I have nothing to fear. I've seen what's waiting for me. I'm not scared of death.' He stroked her hand. 'If only you could have seen what I've seen. Let's enjoy the time I have left, but I don't want any of you to cry for me when I die. I will be in a good place. I even saw the great send off you're going give me! I saw our local church filled with people and lots of yellow flowers. Oh yes, by the way, you're not turning up in a black limo. You're arriving in my lovely lime green Ford! It's true. I've seen it and it makes me happy.'

Leaving the body and seeing the light

Imagine being clinically dead in an operating theatre. You're not supposed to have any brain activity yet there you are floating out of your lifeless body and looking down at what's happening in the room. And you're aware of everything that's going on around you—how the doctors and nurses are trying to resuscitate you and what they're saying. Amazingly, you don't feel any trauma from being separated from your body and there is an all-pervading sense of peace and calm despite the unfolding drama.

Some critics of the concept of near-death experience suggest that what people are really seeing when they are clinically dead is simply the surfacing of stored memories as the brain fires off its last round of electrical impulses. Others suggest that people are merely hallucinating because of administered drugs or a lack of oxygen. But if your brain is being starved of oxygen shouldn't it become confused and your cognitive abilities be impaired? How can you have such clear experiences of what's going on in your environment? And if the near-death experience is just a hallucination created by a dying brain, how is this hallucination so precise?

Suzie's near-death experience, during an operation to remove a cancerous kidney, was disarmingly accurate. Could she have been hallucinating or dredging up old memories when she was declared clinically dead? Yes, she heard the conversation between the doctors standing around her but what was more surprising was that she floated out of the operating theatre and found her husband in a waiting room. She even saw the headline 'Tiananmen Square Massacre' splashed across the front page of the newspaper he was reading.

After visiting her husband, Suzie moved to the next stage of a near-death experience, where people often experience movement, a sense of travelling very quickly up a dark tunnel. She emerged into a beautiful light-filled space where she found her French grandmother waiting for her with open arms. It was the most enchanting reunion and Suzie didn't want to leave the place she was in. But her grandmother lovingly insisted that she had to come back to earth.

'Non, non, ma petite. It's not your time, not yet for many years. And besides, you are going to have a baby girl. Ah, bien sur, you don't know it but yes, you are already enceinte.'

Suzie demanded a pregnancy test as soon as she regained consciousness. Both her husband and her doctor thought she was having a reaction to her medication but when she told her husband where she'd found him reading the paper with news of Tiananmen Square she convinced them she wasn't delusional. The pregnancy test revealed that she was six weeks pregnant. And in due time she gave birth to a baby girl just as her grandmother predicted. Isn't it fascinating how you can have a psychic experience, one that accurately predicts the future, when you are technically dead?

Not everyone has a similar experience to Suzie's, some simply recall seeing their entire life flash in front of them and watching it as though they were watching a movie. This summary of their life may only take moments but it seems timeless. Many people report seeing a light at the end of the tunnel. But each experience is unique and descriptions of what the end of the tunnel looks like vary. Many are greeted by someone they know and find it a comforting and joyous experience.

I had to laugh when a close friend of mine said, 'God, I'd love to have an near-death experience, if I knew I would definitely come back!' Some of us are meant to have an near-death experience and some of us are not. If you're not meant to have one, at least you can always talk to someone who has.

20

I'm Beside Myself

A near-death experience is a beautiful and liberating journey into the Spirit world but it's not to be confused with an out-of-body experience. An out-of-body experience is different because you haven't flat-lined. Out-of-body experiences happen when the astral body drifts up out of your physical body. Most people experience a sensation of feeling light and free as they float above their sleeping body, although some even experience it while they're awake. Perhaps you've experienced something like this yourself? Or maybe your partner or a friend has told you that something like this has happened to them but they didn't understand what was happening.

There's nothing unusual about the process of an out-of-body experience. It happens naturally every night when you slip into a deep sleep. Your astral body projects out and heads for the Spirit realm where you experience your dreams. An out-of-body experience occurs when you haven't fully crossed over into the Spirit realm as you do when you're dreaming and your astral body is momentarily caught in between worlds—it's not in your physical body but it's not in the Spirit world either. While you hover over your body, you're aware that you are in the room, and you can see your sleeping form below you. The reason why you can see things even though your waking mind is asleep is because your soul consciousness is wide awake.

The beautiful thing about an out-of-body experience is that it shows you how strong other states of awareness really are. If you happen to find yourself having an out-of-body experience go with the flow and enjoy it. You don't need to have a near-death experience to validate that your soul really does exist.

I've never forgotten an out-of-body experience I had when I was eleven years old. I had a terrible migraine and I was in a lot of pain, but as I didn't like taking medication I put up with it. While I tossed and turned I could hear my brothers and sisters playing outside. Suddenly I felt a weird slipping sensation and the next thing I knew I was floating above myself. It was incredible. I was actually looking down at myself curled up in a foetal position with my hands cradling my throbbing head. I don't know how long I was out of my body. It felt timeless and then suddenly my body jerked as I jumped back in. The most amazing part of this experience was that the moment I returned I felt a flood of endorphins wash through my brain and the migraine disappeared.

I feel it's important for people to talk about their out-of-body experiences. If you know that others are having the same experiences as you it creates a sense of solidarity. Sharing also helps demystify out-of-body experiences and helps you put them in context. I especially feel it's important for parents to use their sixth sense and tune in and see if their kids are having out-of-body experiences. It can make a huge difference to their children's sleep.

Melissa told me: 'When I was a kid I used to find myself floating up from my body. It scared me because I had a hard time trying to get back into it. I didn't understand what was going on. Sometimes I was too scared to go to sleep because I didn't want it to happen again. It never crossed my mind to tell my parents about it. In hindsight, I wish I had. Maybe they could have helped me move past my fear. When my daughter started having out-of-body experiences she opened up to me and I could help her. It comforted her to know that it was okay to have this experience and that nothing bad would come from it.'

Have you felt a slipping sensation while you're falling asleep? That's the beginning of an out-of-body experience. Maybe you started floating out of your body but something interrupted the process and you quickly returned to your body with a jump or a shudder. Sometimes the impact of returning so quickly feels as if your heart has skipped a beat. I'm often asked, 'Was I about to have a heart attack?' No, you've just come back into your body too quickly, that's all.

Out-of-body experiences aren't restricted to bedtime, they can happen anytime you're napping or sleeping. And sometimes you might end up seeing a little more action than you bargained for.

Recently, I had a fascinating experience. I was hovering over my body and I saw my mum's friend Christina's astral body walking through my bedroom. She walked across the room and I telepathically asked her, 'What are you doing here?'

She looked at me and replied telepathically, 'Oh, it's my health, you know.'

Then she walked over to the venetian blinds in my room and used her fingers to pry the wooden slats open to gaze out at the street.

'I wonder how long I am going to live,' she said without looking at me. Then she walked straight through the blinds and was gone.

I felt my body jump and the next thing I knew I was sitting up in bed. Was I really having an out-of-body experience while Christina's astral body was in my room? No doubt she was dreaming about me for this to happen. How delightful to have this kind of interaction going on while my body was in a gentle sleep. I called Mum the next day and asked after Christina's health. Apparently, she'd been worried about her bad back and other health issues.

If you are lucky enough to have an out-of-body experience, enjoy it. Trust that you are ok and that it's a perfectly natural thing to have happen to you. Out-of-body experiences remind us that there is so much more to our existence than meets the eye. Yes, we are truly multi-dimensional.

21

Frequent Flyers not Required for Where We're Going

One of the more thrilling aspects of working with the sixth sense is that you get to go travelling—astral travelling, which is also what you do when you're having an out-of-body experience. The two states are very similar but what separates them is that you can choose to astral travel, whereas most out-of-body experiences are spontaneous. You can control and direct astral travel (also known as projection), so where you go, and what you do, is up to you.

Imagine what it would feel like to be able to visit a friend in a different country while relaxing in your own lounge room. Or to explore uncharted territory in the Spirit realm. There are so many benefits to working with altered states of consciousness. All you have to do is think outside the square and let your soul roam free. Well, part of it anyway; the part called the astral body. It's the section of your soul that spontaneously projects out during out-of-body experiences and dreaming. Wouldn't it be fantastic to do it at will—to project your astral self and be free to travel anywhere in the world? Well, now you can. But before I show you how to astral travel, I want to share a story with you.

Years ago my brother Joe woke up in the middle of the night feeling thirsty. While contemplating whether he should leave his warm bed to get a drink, he glanced through the open door and suddenly saw Nonna, our grandmother, standing in the hallway.

'I've gotta be dreaming,' he told himself. Nonna lived overseas, but here she was smiling and waving at him. Eventually he got out of bed and as he ventured down the hallway Nonna followed him into the kitchen. After gulping down a glass of water and pinching himself several times he was dismayed to find that Nonna didn't dematerialise. She just kept waving to him.

'Nonna?' he asked. 'It is you, isn't it?' She smiled but didn't answer and followed him into his room before waving goodbye.

When Joe got up in the morning he found my mother crying after receiving a call informing her that Nonna had just died. By astral travelling Nonna was able to visit Joe in soul-person form. Having seen Nonna's happy face only hours earlier made a world of difference to Joe.

If you think you haven't astral travelled before, think again. Astral travelling is a natural process for the soul. Would it surprise you to hear if you have a catnap during the day, that while you're dreaming, you could end up astral travelling locally instead of on the astral realm? Say you dreamed that you were at work and there was a commotion about your boss quitting—you saw, heard and felt everything as if it was really happening. The next day you turn up to work and find out your boss has resigned. This isn't necessarily a prophetic dream per se, but the result of you unknowingly astral travelling.

How to astral travel

Sit down, close your eyes and relax. Take a nice deep breath and slowly exhale. Keep breathing deeply until you are very, very relaxed. Ask your guides to protect you while you're astral travelling, or you can say a protective prayer or mantra.

Bring down a white light over and through your entire body. Take your awareness inside you and visualise your astral self stepping out a metre in front of you. Even though your physical eyes are closed, you can see the room with your astral eyes.

Now let yourself float up to the ceiling and look down at yourself sitting. Then let yourself rise up through the ceiling and sit on top of the roof and look up at the sky, then down onto the street, and survey what's going on. Practice doing this technique for a few weeks until you're comfortable with it.

When you are in your 'trainee' period don't be surprised if on the odd occasion you feel like you haven't returned properly into your body. If you feel slightly out of whack, or out of sync with your body, take a few breaths and state your intention to realign your astral body with your physical body. You'll be back in sync with yourself in no time at all.

When you feel you're up to moving to the next stage and doing some astral travel further afield, project your astral body into a friend's place and see what they are up to. (It might be a good idea to arrange this with your friend first.)

When you're ready, come back and open your eyes. Check with your friend to verify the accuracy of your remote viewing.

I like to advise people that until you understand how other realms of reality work you should take your time with each step. And don't use drugs to help you astral travel. I know a lot of shamanistic practices involve using medicinal plants to connect with the Spirit world, but these practitioners spend a lot of time purifying their energies beforehand. Don't let enthusiasm make you rush in to realms you are not prepared for. It's important to protect your energies so you know you're always going to have a safe trip no matter where you go. If you find yourself somewhere that's dark, focus on your physical body and state your intention to immediately return back into sync with it. Or ask your guides to lift you away from this dark place and take you to a safer place in the Spirit world.

Allowing the sixth sense to guide you while you are astral travelling ensures that you are always safe and in control. It helps make your journey a real pleasure.

22

There's no Time Like the Right Time

The sense of freedom that comes from being in two places at once is exciting. Your physical body and your astral body are in two different places, yet they're still connected. But these are not the only things you can get in sync with. Don't you just love that ah-ha moment when you join the dots between two separate events? This is what Carl Jung called synchronicity. It happens when two separate events, with no apparent causal connection, reveal that a meaningful relationship exists between them. Synchronised moments are simply awe-inspiring because you get to see exactly how interconnected the world really is.

Many people don't recognise the threads that tie events together because they're not paying attention. Moments of synchronicity can be so simple that you may not always make the connection between two events, especially if you have never been taught to do so. Perhaps you have put down links between two unrelated events as mere coincidence.

I took my dog Bodo for a walk one morning and I stopped by a lovely cluster of trees and asked nature for some healing. I received the most beautiful healing energy and I returned home feeling effervescent. I went to my computer and opened my email and found that someone had sent me a chain email offering healing from Saint Teresa with a prayer. The previous night I had caught up with some healing students for dinner and we had been talking about premonitions and a student told me about her mum and her connection with Saint Teresa. That's simple synchronicity for you!

Unrelated events that occur simultaneously by chance are called coincidences. But when such unrelated events seem connected by a theme, pattern or even a symbol, I don't believe that's all they are. I believe they happen for a reason and are synchronicities which we will become aware of once we start following the threads, joining the unseen dots. It's not complicated. It's actually a very elegant equation—the connection between the inner and outer world.

A meaningful relationship exists between you and everything you draw into your life. All you need to do is spend a few minutes being in the moment. Take a deep breath, relax and clear your mind. Look at where you are. Look at your outer world and become aware of the moment you are in. Soon you'll start seeing synchronicity happening all around you.

I find that instances of synchronicity take place when life is 'flowing'. I use these moments as my yardstick for how I am travelling on my life's journey.

I remember waking up one morning feeling melancholy. Time was running out. My guide had told me that the person

I loved was coming back into my life in August. It was late July and I had been told by friends that he was thinking of marrying his girlfriend. How could my guides get it so wrong? I was losing faith. Perhaps I was deluding myself.

The bleak winter weather didn't help my mood and as I stepped into the shower I asked Upstairs to give me a sign that the prediction was true. They did. Literally! They showed me a number plate with MIK on it. Seeing this would be a sign of their accuracy. I said, 'You've got to be kidding?' But my guide was adamant. 'You will see this number plate within the next half hour.'

I dressed and was about to leave for work when I got a call from my son Tristan's school asking me to swing by and drop off something for him. It wasn't on my normal route and would make me late for work but I had to do it. I started checking out every single number plate on the way but I couldn't see a single one starting with the letter M. It was crazy—trying to find this combination was one in a million. I even nearly ran off the road a few times in my ridiculous bid to find a number plate with MIK on it!

All the parking spots outside the school were taken and I double-parked between two cars, dropped off Tristan's things and got back behind the wheel.

'This is insane,' I told myself.

I sat quietly for a minute wrestling with my mind. Logic won and I decided there wasn't any point in looking at any more number plates. I started the engine and edged forwards a metre. Despite my resolve I decided to look at just one more number plate. I moved another half a metre forwards and quickly looked to my left. There it was—MIK—on a truck I'd double-parked less than a metre away from!

This was synchronicity. Spirit had it all planned out beautifully—the call from the school, having to take a different route to work, having to double-park and finally seeing the MIK number plate. I could hear my guides laughing. The man in question came back into my social circle that August and we got back together at Christmas time.

Every time I feel synchronicity happening I know that I am exactly where I need to be, that I am right on cue. Included in these moments are some of the most profound experiences I've had. Why not let your sixth sense help you discover synchronicity?

23

Alchemy

It's those magical moments when things fall into place that make you feel like you're on top of the game. The fantastic intuitive tool called the sixth sense can enrich your life in so many ways—if you let it. If you leave it alone, it will lay fallow in the recesses of your mind. I've always found that the most magical light-bulb moments come immediately after my sixth sense has kicked in. It will artfully connect two pieces of your personal puzzle, and it's during these reflective or insightful moments that you end up creating a little personal alchemy.

Alchemy is the art of turning common metals into gold. The alchemy of life is about transforming the most precious of all resources—ourselves. The sixth sense plays a vital role in this transformation. With a little work, you can emerge from your inner cocoon a beautiful, enlightened, butterfly. Gone are the base aspects of yourself like fears, doubts and restrictive beliefs. They've been replaced by self-awareness, self-assurance and a strong connection with your higher self. Personal alchemy is about becoming the highest aspect of your soul's potential—and that's a sight of rare beauty to behold.

Susana felt this happen to her. 'As a child I felt unloved. I grew up believing I had to prove myself to everybody. I became whatever people wanted me to be because that's what people-pleasers do. I couldn't even say no to my own mother. She would say, "I'm coming over and bringing your nieces" and even if I didn't want her to come because I was tired or busy, I couldn't bring myself to refuse. I put her needs before my own because I felt guilty. I wouldn't say no to anybody because deep down inside I felt they'd judge me as being selfish and uncooperative. I know this was ridiculous, that it was all in my head, but that was my reality. I honestly felt they were judging me.

'During my last parapsychology class I had a breakthrough. For the first time in my life I truly connected to my higher self. I heard this part of me, my sixth sense, say very, very clearly, "You have nothing to prove." It reverberated through my whole body. Something shifted within me and I felt truly liberated. It was like someone had taken a huge burden off me; I was free to be me. I actually started crying because I saw myself walking off the people-pleaser stage. You've got no idea of how much energy it took to constantly prove myself to everyone.

'A week later Mum called to say she was coming over and bringing the family and as usual expected me to do lunch for everyone. I love my family but bending over to make them happy at my expense wasn't working any more. I realised that by accommodating their needs all I was really doing was trying to make myself acceptable enough to be loved by them. The only time I could say no was when my body started reacting and making me feel sick, so I could legitimately say, "No, Mum, I can't because I'm sick" and I'd go to bed. I can't tell you how many times that happened. Crazy, my body made me sick so I could honour what I needed.

'This time I mustered up the courage and said no without feeling guilty. God, it felt so liberating. I risked their disapproval and in the process I managed to gain self-acceptance.

'My sixth sense was right. I know that connecting to my higher self transformed my life.'

The sixth sense is the part of you that helps you unravel the mystery of your own life. What a real blessing this is. Do you want to know what the secret to happiness is in this mixed-up world? It's feeling the uplifting sense of confidence and wellbeing that comes with being at peace with who and what you are. If there's a part of you that you need to let go of—a fear, a restrictive belief or pattern—use your sixth sense to shed some light on the issue. There's a wonderful perceptual clarity that comes from working with your sixth sense. Why not use it to create a little alchemy today?

24

Everyday Miracles

A little bit of personal alchemy goes a long way. It goes even further when you work in a little magic to change the lives of others.

When life gets on top of us we tend to want to run and hide. Or, at least we try to. It's during times like this that we cry out for a miracle to make life wonderful again. I don't know about you but I feel a little jaded when no miracle appears on the horizon. But when you're being tossed around by a massive storm which leaves a pile of debris in your path it's easy to lose sight of everyday miracles. It's even easier to convince yourself that miracles don't happen—at least not to you.

Miracles don't always come on cue but they do happen. The universe does listen to your prayers but it's waiting for the right time to send you its blessings. Sometimes a miracle arrives without fanfare, so you don't see it in all its glory. At other times it arrives in the most unlikely manner.

Anne is a beautiful person. She's a caring healer and massage therapist, a former student of mine who throws her heart and soul into her work. Anne's six-month-old grandson Kiernan was born with a fused skull which was going to require an operation. It so happened that on the day I went to see Anne for a remedial massage her grandson was with her and Anne asked if I could work on him.

Kiernan had a cold so his mother had cancelled his specialist appointment to have a final brain scan and book the operation. Since birth little Kiernan had been having monthly brain scans to monitor his fused skull. Each scan showed no growth, where they should have been some. Kiernan's mum entered the healing room carrying a gorgeous and happy little boy. She took one look at me and gave me the strangest look.

'I know you,' she said, her eyes carefully scanning my face.

I couldn't recall meeting her and suggested that maybe she'd seen a photo.

Turning to her mother-in-law she said, 'Anne, this is really strange, but I do know her.' She went silent for a minute then exclaimed, 'That's where I've seen you! I dreamed about you a few months ago. You said you were here to work on Kiernan. You healed him and he didn't have to have the operation.'

Anne and I did a spiritual healing on Kiernan focusing our attention on helping his skull to grow. Working with your sixth sense can give you an edge when you're doing any form of energetic healing. You're able to tune in and get intuitive impressions of what needs to be done. You can get a clearer picture of your client's karma so you can understand the lessons behind the illness. Having this insight can make a significant difference not only in how you work with people, but also to how they'll respond to the healing, and how they will deal with any issues from it.

Children born with medical problems carry a strong karmic lesson from a previous life. Their health crisis is part of their soul's journey. When you're dealing with a strong karmic medical condition it's wise to recognise that the karma has set the boundaries—recovery or death. If it's in the person's karma to experience the full gamut of the disease, then they will. Any healing they get will help them along but it doesn't necessarily mean they'll be cured. This makes it hard for people who are hoping for a miracle. How do you override strong karma?

Kiernan lay on the massage table, smiling peacefully while we worked. I used my sixth sense to see if it was possible to help him resolve the karmic energy behind his condition. I also checked to see what the lesson of his illness was for his mother and grandmother. Health issues aren't always about the patient alone; they're often about teaching family and friends as well. What did his mother need to learn from this experience? What did Anne need to learn? And as his mother had had a premonition that I was instrumental in Kiernan's recovery, there was definitely a lesson for me too.

Two weeks later Anne called me. 'Sue you wouldn't believe it,' she said unable to contain her excitement. 'They took Kiernan for the scan. The specialist was amazed. He said it was impossible but Kiernan's skull has actually grown two centimetres! They don't have to operate any more. We got our miracle.'

Sometimes miracles aren't as dramatic as this. They can also weave into your life in very subtle ways, gradually alleviating your misfortune. In these cases, because the change you'd hoped for comes slowly or in stages, you may not recognise that you have received your miracle. Always remember to work with your sixth sense. It will help you to recognise miracles by giving you an insight into the time, place and even the form they may appear in. Anne's family were hoping the doctors were going to perform the miracle. Instead, Anne herself had a hand in creating it.

25

The Sixth Sense in Future Tense

As much as we wish for miracles, sometimes the lesson is about letting go and going with the flow of life.

At twenty-two I had a dream I've never forgotten. I remember waking up in the stifling heat of a summer night with my heart racing and a thin film of sweat on my brow. As I tried to settle myself down, I went over and over the dream I'd just had in my mind, trying to figure it out. I had dreamed of Tony, my mother's godson. He was surrounded by an enormous ring of fire and he appeared to be very angry. He stood there, like a trapped animal, not knowing how to get out. On the outside of the circle of fire, I could see his parents crying—their cries like melancholic sobs. I could sense their despair and, intuitively, I knew something was very wrong in his life. I woke and lay there in the dark trying to force myself to go back to sleep but the image of Tony, trapped in that ring of fire, haunted me beyond sunrise.

I don't know why I dreamed of Tony. I hadn't seen or spoken to him during the three years I'd been away studying at university. When I got up in the morning I told Mum about the dream but neither of us could make any sense of it. Still, a feeling of foreboding remained. This dream embedded itself deeply into my mind and I couldn't stop thinking about it.

One week later Tony was dead. He died instantly when his car crashed into a pole during a wild thunderstorm. It was then that the dream took on meaning.

That is often the trouble with premonitions, especially when the vision comes in a dream. Not all premonition dreams are spelled out in big black letters, so you can't always fully understand their meaning. The one thing you know for certain is that this kind of dream feels different to your other dreams. You can't quite put your finger on why it's different, but it is. Unlike other dreams, which fade from your mind within minutes of waking up, this one lingers on through the day and into the next. It's the kind of dream that leaves you feeling a little unsettled, as though you're missing a vital piece of information. Why can't you forget it? After all, it's only a dream, isn't it?

Later, the huge question created by your dream is finally answered and you look back and say, 'Why didn't I get it? If I had, maybe things would have turned out differently?' It's easy to beat yourself up for not acting on a premonition, or simply not recognising it when you had it, like I did after I heard about Tony's death. My having that premonition didn't change the outcome for him, so why did I have it? Why did I get the premonition and not his mother or father who might have warned him to take it easy because they understood the significance of the dream?

The simple fact is my premonition was never intended to change his path, because it was his time to go. The message was for me, to tell me that I could see things that could and would happen to get me to start paying attention. Talk about pulling no punches, it certainly got me listening to spirits loud and clear!

So, yes we can see into the future. But, just because you can see the future it doesn't mean you can always control it. Sometimes we can change things and sometimes we can't.

Since that day I've had some truly wonderful premonitions of people and events that were to come into my life; and they did. It's kind of comforting to know a little piece of what the future holds for you; there's a sense of security that comes with knowing what to expect.

Premonitions are not always easy to interpret, but if you practise opening yourself up to the experience, life takes on a whole new meaning.

For some of us the sixth sense feels like a natural part of our essence, flowing harmoniously with our other tactile senses. It can be strong or it can come in occasional flashes when you least expect it. I, like many of you, was born with this sixth sense but chose not to turn it on because I preferred to stick to reason. That was until my premonition of Tony, the beginning of a long line of visitors from the other side, and my gradual acceptance that the sixth sense was a very real part of me. It's a very real part of you too.

26

It's Called Animal Instinct for a Reason

We're not the only ones who have premonitions or see Spirit. Our pets have the sixth sense too.

Several years ago Jerry came to stay with my family for a week and ended up staying a year and a half. Jerry Dog, as she was affectionately known, was a titan—a mix of Great Dane and English mastiff who quickly made herself at home, even excavating large holes in the back yard for her comfort. When Bodo, my small champagne coloured moodle first saw Jerry he went crazy. Having a giant treading his turf ruffled his fur no end.

Both dogs loved their walk around the lake. Bodo was a kid-magnet drawing gasps and pats from adoring kiddies, while Jerry had a slightly different affect on people. Grown men would literally jump out of their skin at the sight of this huge, fearsome dog. 'She's really a gentle soul,' I'd explain, but it fell on deaf ears.

One day Bodo decided to start sleeping next to Jerry, which was unusual as Bodo hated sleeping outdoors. He did this every night for two weeks which baffled us. The kids thought it was the humid summer nights that kept him outdoors, but Bodo had a different reason.

Jerry was nearly twelve years old and was riddled with an inoperable cancer. Although losing some weight, she was still very strong. I should know, she literally ripped my arm out of its socket every time we'd start a walk. One stormy afternoon I came home to find Jerry Dog languishing. She stood there with her tongue hanging out and I knew her time had come. She walked towards me on unsteady legs and I patted her and sent a telepathic message that it was ok to go 'home', then I took her inside. Bodo was beside himself, knowing exactly what was going on. His sixth sense had told him weeks earlier that Jerry's time with us was ending and that's why he'd taken to spending so much time with her, even snuggling up to her outside at night.

After Jerry was gone Bodo continued running around the yard looking for her. I remember my sister watching him a week after Jerry had passed, and remarking on how he seemed to be barking at something in front of him, only there wasn't anything there. 'Is he hoping Jerry comes home?' she asked.

'No,' I said. 'Jerry's Spirit is here, she's visiting and he is playing with her.'

Pets are psychic so please don't underestimate their ability. Listen to them. You might be pleasantly surprised by what they have to say.

27

When Oscar Tried to Save Nicole

Humans might pride themselves on being logical and clever, but an animal's instinctive nature runs circles over our logic every time. Ask any switched on pet owner and they'll tell you that their animal has an amazing sixth sense.

Have you ever noticed how quickly pets pick up on your moods and how they try to comfort you when you're feeling sad or lonely? They can also sense danger and they can see Spirit. So the next time you notice your dog barking or your cat meowing at a corner in the room, or looking as if they're following an imaginary friend around the house, tune in. You'll find that they're actually communicating with your Spirit visitors.

What's truly remarkable about pets is their ability to sense illness and disease in people. Nicole, a student of mine, told me a really interesting story.

'Months before I was diagnosed with cancer my dog Oscar used to jump on my lap and constantly nuzzle against my breast, which was odd because he never used to touch that part of my body. Oscar kept on doing it day after day and while he was doing it he'd give me a funny look, as if he was trying to tell me something, only at the time I didn't get it.'

A year later Nicole happened to be watching a current affairs program that ran a feature on a clinic in England where a doctor kept a dog in the surgery. The dog could sense cancer in a patient and proved to be right every time. The doctor remarked that he felt dogs could do this because of their keen sense of smell. But smelling a disease is one thing, trying to warn a human is another.

Oscar kept nuzzling at Nicole's diseased breast, and kept at it because Oscar wanted Nicole to pay attention. Oscar's sixth sense was unfortunately right—Nicole had cancer and her dog had done his best to tell her.

Next time your pet is acting strangely, tune in and see if you can sense what they're trying to tell you.

28

Getting a Grip

Is getting premonitions your forte? If not, what's your unique gift? Do you think it is clairvoyance, clairaudience or clairsentience? Perhaps it's mediumship or astral travel? Maybe your gift lies in healing or helping people with intuitive guidance? There is so much scope to work with when it comes to the sixth sense.

To a beginner, it can be daunting to find out you are starting with a blank canvas. You'd prefer a colour-by-numbers exercise, with a picture to guide you towards the perfect end product. If only it was that easy!

When beginners ask me 'How will I find out what I am going to be good at?' I tell them, 'Part of the journey is to find your unique gifts for yourself. Start with the blank canvas, open your senses, and see where they take you.' Exploring is the fun part. Eventually you will find which modality suits you best. How will you do that? Simply by feeling it!

I like to teach my students a little of all the sixth-sense gifts. I find it helps them hone in on what's right for them. I usually start them off with clairvoyance. It's a great starting point because you get to work the third-eye chakra, your intuitive centre. After working their way through the different sensory modalities most people quickly find out which one resonates with them. Give yourself the opportunity and time to explore them all. Don't dismiss something because you think it's too hard or that you're never going to be as good as someone else. You might surprise yourself if you stay open.

Look for what resonates with you. If clairvoyance doesn't sing for you, then set it aside and try your hand at clairaudience and so on. When you find which modality speaks to you, spend time exploring its different facets. For example, if it's clairvoyance, start playing with different images. Try visualising images in your mind's eye while your physical eyes are closed. Then try getting an image in your mind's eye while your eyes are open. You can try getting messages as symbols, pictures or even moving images. Try your hand at all of them. With time it gets easier to work with your gift because you become much more relaxed. This is why practice is invaluable.

I remember the first time my teacher threw me in the deep end. We were at a stall at a psychic fair. 'You can set up over there,' she pointed to the edge of the stall. 'I want you to do both Spirit-guide drawings and psychic readings today. It'll be great practice.'

I looked at her as if to say, 'Are you insane? Me, do this all day long? What if I trip up?'

She must have read my mind. 'You'll be fine,' she reassured me.

The morning passed by quietly. I didn't have a single customer. My teacher came over and said, 'Sue, you're blocking the flow.

Relax and trust that you can do it. I wouldn't have brought you here if I didn't think you were up to it.'

I relaxed and let go of my doubts about being good enough. Five minutes later my first client arrived. Of course, my mind went completely blank! My customer was just looking at me waiting for something, anything. I began thinking I should crawl under a rock. But then I felt the presence of one of my guides, they were touching my shoulders and this encouraged me. I took a deep breath, closed my eyes, focused on my third eye and waited for images to surface. At that point my sixth sense kicked in.

How I got through that first customer I don't know but soon people were lining up. I heard someone say, 'Hey, the lady doing the guide drawings is great.' I even had one of the other psychics turn up to get a reading because she'd heard about the excellent job I was doing. The more readings I did, the easier it became. I felt my confidence rising. The information was flowing through me beautifully and I wasn't making mistakes.

If you feel that mediumship resonates with you, start practising by trying to feel the presence of guides or special family members in Spirit. Open your senses to their personalities. Is there something in the atmosphere that reminds you of a particular person? A fragrance or smell? Ask Spirit to touch your face or shoulder to let you know they're around. Make yourself comfortable with the idea of having Spirit surrounding you. And even if you can't see or feel them to begin with, just keep talking to them and be open to their ways of communicating. A lot of mediums start with clairvoyance, getting images in their head about who's around them. It's a fantastic way to begin. Don't let mistakes bother you. It's okay to make mistakes. I can't stress it enough. It's actually part of the process. So persevere!

Be careful of your expectations. Just because you're interested in a particular sixth-sense gift, doesn't necessarily mean you're a natural. Sometimes what you think, and what you feel, can be different. Instead of thinking a gift is right, feel it and resonate with it. This way you don't end up chasing your tail. You are born with certain gifts. You might be a fantastic clairvoyant and conscious medium but if the door to trance mediumship is karmically closed to you, it won't open no matter how much time and effort you put into it. If Spirit doesn't want to open the door to a particular gift, then it won't. This isn't a vendetta against you. Your guides appreciate your dedication in pursuing your gifts, but they are aware of the bigger picture. If they see that your destiny lies in another area, that's the gift they will work on with you. They know in the long run where your gift will take you.

It's your choice, of course, but let your inner-self guide you. Remember, no single modality is better than another—they're all fantastic gifts. Some people will develop a whole range of intuitive skills while others will develop only one sixth-sense gift, and that's ok. It's your personal journey, not a competition, so focus on what is working for you. The right door will always open.

29

Keeping Tight with the Boss

You have the sixth sense. But sometimes you need a little encouragement from the right source to show you how talented you really are. Instead of letting your rational mind get in the way, why not let the truly inspirational and amazing part of you do the talking? That's what your higher self is. It's the part of you that is brimming with insight and it makes the best choices.

Some people talk about the higher self without any real spiritual understanding of exactly what it is. The higher self is the eternal part of you that knows your truth. It knows where you are going. It has all the answers because it's holding your soul's blueprint. If you listen to your higher self you'll get all the insight and inspiration you want and need.

You've probably connected with your higher self for brief moments without even knowing it. Quite unexpectedly at a major crossroad, or even in a quiet moment of solitude, you may have inadvertently flicked on the switch and your higher self sent you an important message. You probably didn't realise this was happening. I didn't when I was eleven years old.

It was a beautiful summer day, not a cloud in the sky and we were having so much fun at the beach. I was wading in the salty water with a friend, resting my arms on a floaty. For some unknown reason I became aware of a lady standing at the far end of the beach pool. She was tall and slender, and her wet hair hung in long tendrils. A part of me said, 'You're going to be okay now. She will help you.' I had no idea what this meant.

Moments later, my friend lost her footing and pushed down on my shoulders to keep herself afloat. My plastic floaty dislodged and before I knew it I was under the water and I couldn't breathe. Somehow, I didn't panic. A film began running in my head which contained snippets of my life—shots of me at home, me walking to school, playing with my sisters, talking to my parents and even looking up at the Milky Way at night. It was surreal and timeless and I was strangely happy and content. I was at peace with everything.

The next thing I knew I was lying on the sand. I don't remember being pulled out of the water. I remember my eyes were slightly blurred from being irritated by too much salt water. I saw my sisters and my friend hovering around me, concern etched on their tanned faces. And the lady I had seen before was kneeling by my side, asking me if I was all right. She explained she had resuscitated me. In that brief moment before the incident, I had connected to that part of me that knew what would happen. My higher self was right—I was ok.

The reason most of us are unaware of the higher self is because our logical, rational self shuts it out. It lies dormant within us waiting to be activated and come into its own. Isn't it crazy to think we're living life with an essential part of us shut behind a closed door? The part of us behind the door is the remarkable half; it accepts us unconditionally, sending love without judgement. The part of us that's on the loose is the ego, constantly at war with itself, constantly demanding attention and shadow boxing. Wouldn't life be so much easier if we could open up and welcome the soul-aspect that already talks to us in our dreams and moves through the Spirit world?

A valuable tool for doing this is meditation. Meditation works by inducing a connective state, a bridge between the lower and higher self. It achieves this by changing your brainwave patterns to allow a deeper connection with yourself. It gives you the opportunity to look at your thoughts, your feelings and your vision. It allows you to see what is limiting you. It also lets you open, activate and clear the chakras.

One of the many effective meditation techniques you can work with is the eastern-style mantra meditation. A mantra is a single word, phrase, symbol or sound that creates a powerful sacred invocation. The object of this type of meditation is to focus on a repetitive sound or thought, which enables you to transcend the ego and move into a deep state of relaxation.

Another effective technique to get in touch with your higher self is visualisation, where you imagine such activities as a walk along the beach or in a forest to evoke deep emotional responses that in turn can help you identify issues stored in your chakras. Creative visualisation is a lot like daydreaming. It's a dream that can also be used to create an image in your mind of things you want to manifest in your life.

Connecting with your higher self is one of the best moves you can make because it helps you feel complete.

30

You've got Mind-mail!

Despite being strange, even frustratingly illogical, dreams are important. What makes them so important is that they are live broadcasts from your soul. The bizarre scenes in your dreams hold important messages for you. Each dream is unique, and serves a purpose for you. Take advantage of this superb inner resource.

The first thing you need to realise is that all dreams have a purpose, whether that is to process and release daily concerns or to deliver inner messages. Think of a dream as a story written in the symbolic language of the soul. At first, like any language, it can appear complicated but once you've learned how to read symbols, no dream will ever be a mystery again.

The second thing you need to understand is that your higher self and your Spirit guides utilise dreams to get some quality time with you, to draw your attention to the things that matter. It could be finding vision and inspiration, satisfying a need, dealing with a repressed emotion or helping you to confront your fears. Dreams are also the perfect place to reconnect with the dearly departed.

My sister Lena once dreamed about our dad. He died in 2001 and she hadn't dreamed about him in over four years. At first she thought, no, this is just a dream, but when he started speaking to her, she knew it was real. She said he was happy and content. He was smiling about the family and she got the impression something good was going to happen. He said, 'Watch the chickens.' Then he hugged her. Lena was overwhelmed by the warmth of his hug because it felt solid and real. She remembers thinking, 'This is too real to be a dream.' Surprisingly, that same night I also dreamed of Dad. I told Lena that in dreams 'chickens' means that there are good times coming soon. This symbol explained Dad's message of happiness.

You can also enmesh dreams. Yes, merge into each others' dreams by having the same dream at the same time. I love this story that my friend Michelle told me about her and her husband Steve's experience.

'Steve and I would have the same dreams—mostly soon after we were married. On our wedding day the priest had explained that at some point in the ceremony our auras became enmeshed and that for a while Steve and I would be having the same dreams. I don't know if this was the power of suggestion, but our dreams were the same in every way.

'The other thing that happened a lot was that we'd both wake up all of a sudden in the middle of the night to see the biggest spiders hanging from our ceiling. I'd scream, Steve would see it, we'd jump out of bed, hit the lights and then all of a sudden, nothing was there.'

Dreams can also act as a clearing house for the subconscious mind. Melissa dreamed she'd walked into her grandparent's kitchen through the back door. 'I saw my grandmother, who has passed over, standing in the adjacent dining room. She gave me a hug and I could feel her as though she were solid. We then walked upstairs to the last bedroom that was set up for an internal garage sale. The tables had sale items. We were walking around talking about what I was up to with spiritual healing. After we left the room, a big heavy door closed behind us.

'We returned downstairs. I could hear someone's voice calling out, sounding like Dad, so we went back upstairs to look for him. The first heavy door opened a little and I had to hold it open for a moment before entering. I saw a shrivelled, dehydrated woman lying on the bed and I instinctively grabbed her in my arms and took her out of the bedroom and down to the kitchen. By the time I got there she had become hydrated. I asked her, "Who are you?"

'She couldn't remember, but she had been taken there for shelter and nobody had come back for her. At that moment I was thinking, that's my story. I was taken to my grandparents' house for shelter at the age of thirteen because of what was happening at home. The woman had been in the same bedroom I stayed in all those years ago.'

When she woke up Melissa realised that this dream was giving her the emotional healing she needed to resolve a deep-seated childhood abandonment issue.

If you've experienced a trauma that's left you feeling overwhelmed it will end up being stored in the subconscious mind. These repressed emotions will create blocks that stem the flow of healthy energy and can eventually form the basis of an illness or disease. Your dreams help you to attend to these matters and heal emotionally before they create a physical problem.

Other dreams have a deeper, spiritual connotation. This is when we enter the Spirit world and become available to message-dreams and prophetic dreams. Every night when you sleep, the astral body, which is connected to you by a silver etheric cord, slips across to the other side. Once you are in this sound sleeping state the subconscious and your soul begin talking to you through symbols.

Let's look at how a dream symbol can work. A house usually symbolises you. Look at the size and state of the house and where it's located and it will start to reveal things about you. Look at the rooms. Each room represents a different part of your life. Being in a kitchen represents your attitude towards self-nurture. Bedrooms represent relationships or putting an issue to bed. The bathroom is where you wash away restrictive thoughts and feelings. Walking downstairs is symbolic of going into a deeper subconscious issue. Walking upstairs means you're seeing things from the super-consciousness, your higher self consciousness.

Even the predominant colours in the rooms have a special meaning. For example, if you're sitting alone in a red-coloured living room it can suggest you need to initiate some social action. If you dream that you're having restless sleep in a blue-coloured bedroom it can indicate you need to put an issue to do with communicating or expressing your truth 'to bed', or that you need healing. If you're having a shower in a yellow-coloured bathroom it can mean you're releasing issues to do with self-empowerment, or you have to stop thinking so much and let your feelings or heart have a say.

What kind of symbols keep popping up in your dreams? Consider what a symbol means to you. A snake can be interpreted in a number of ways: for some it represents healing or transformation, but for others it signals danger. Symbols can be culturally specific so you have to look at what a symbol means to you personally.

If you want to interpret a dream write it out, then underline the main symbols and write down your emotional association to that symbol. String the symbols and emotions together and you'll get a thread to help you interpret the bigger message.

You can also look at the themes of your dreams and types of dreams you are having. For example, the theme of all flying dreams is to inspire you to rise to new heights, while the theme of any kind of falling dream is either to help you deal with feeling inadequate, or to tell you that life is trying to trip you up. Any dream involving the theme of water explores your emotional-self. If you're standing by the beach and a massive tidal wave is heading your way, your soul is letting you know that you're feeling emotionally overwhelmed, regardless of whether or not your rational mind is saying, 'I'm ok'.

Some dreams are designed to help you clear a backlog of unresolved fears and traumas embedded in your subconscious. In a way you could say that these dreams act as down time for emotional repair. The symbols in this kind of dream help you reconstruct an experience stored in your long-term memory that needs to be released. Triggering the original sensations of an unresolved issue gives you the opportunity to review the experience in a non-threatening dream-state environment so you can facilitate your own healing.

Other dreams, such as lucid or prophetic dreams, take you on a journey through a Spirit world. Here you can find inspiration, or the answers to pressing problems, get spiritual guidance from your guides and even take a trip through the time tunnel into the future.

Dreams aren't a meaningless kaleidoscope of surreal images floating around in your head. They play an important role in conveying messages to you from your higher self.

31

Dream Catcher

Your sixth sense is working while you sleep so make the most of it and find out what your dreams mean. They're a lot easier to understand than you think. Once you get a handle on some central themes I'm sure you will find it easier to categorise dreams and decode them. Here is a list of the most common dream themes.

Daily clearance dream

This is when you mull over your day. It helps you to sort out what experiences need to be held onto and which ones can be filed away. Once this is sorted you can go into a deeper dream state. For example, if you've been thinking about an important meeting that's happening the next day, you'll probably sift through all your ideas and expectations during your daily clearance dream.

Prophetic dreams

A prophetic or psychic dream shows you the future. Sometimes what you've seen happens later in real life or, if not, it may evoke a feeling of deja vu if you find yourself in a similar environment or situation.

Teaching dreams

This happens when you wake up, go back to sleep, and then resume a dream where you left off. You were meant to finish it as it contains an important message your soul doesn't want you to miss.

Lesson/repeat dreams

If you ignore a problem you'll end up dreaming about it—over and over again. The same theme will play out over weeks or months, sometimes years, until the penny drops. Once you've dealt with the problem in your waking mind, the repeat dream automatically stops.

Jenny frequently dreamed about her co-worker Martha. 'She was a little difficult to get along with. I dreamt that the two of us were wearing matching jumpsuits and we jumped out of a plane without parachutes. Even though we knew we were about to die, we were doing acrobatic moves. Finally it hit me that I was in trouble, and I thought that if I landed feet first, I would be all right, and I was. When I woke up I realised it related to the dance we were all doing for Martha. Then the dreams stopped.'

Releasing dreams

Dream time is release time. If you're not dealing with an issue, you can confront it by taking action in a dream. A dream can act as a trigger by getting you to think about the problem so that you can release it later on.

I really wanted to win millions. Finally, I dreamed I did and it felt marvellous. I ran around doing everything I wanted to do. Then I woke up. It was only a dream but I was okay with it because I finally got to feel what it felt like to experience the joy of winning, even if it was only for a few hours.

Answer dreams

You've heard the term 'to sleep on it'. What a fantastic idea. Why not let your dreams give you the perfect answer to your problems? The Danish physicist Niels Bohr discovered the structure of atoms after dreaming about a sun made of burning gas which had planets, attached by thin filaments, spinning around it.

Forty years ago when Grace was living in a small mountain village, her five-year-old daughter, Angela, fell seriously ill and the doctor said she was going to die. Grace dreamed she walked into a doctor's room and he said, 'Write down the names of these herbs. It is important to remember these step-by-step instructions on how to process them.'

Dawn broke. Grace woke up her husband and said she was off to pick herbs to make medicine for Angela.

'Are you crazy?' he said.

She made the potion and administered it hourly. By lunchtime relatives had gathered at the house, shaking their heads at her desperate attempt to heal Angela. But later on Angela started coughing up small balls of mucus and blood and by evening she was well again.

Past-life recall

Have you ever heard someone sleep-talking in an unfamiliar or different language? They could be having a past-life recall in a dream. When you dream about being in medieval Europe or Ancient Rome, it could be because you lived there once and are now sorting through some old issues that need resolving.

I had heard Tristan crying out in pain in the middle of the night. I found him sitting up in bed rubbing his leg.

'It hurts,' he said. 'I had a dream I was a knight and I was in this big battle and someone stabbed my leg with his sword. It felt so real. It's still hurting.'

It made sense to me because since the age of four Tristan had been fascinated with medieval knights. It's not uncommon to feel a strong pull to a certain place or time in history where you once lived.

Interference dream

An interference dream occurs when the outside world encroaches on your dream-state, for example, when the sound of a bell ringing in your dream-state is actually the phone ringing in the other room and you've incorporated the noise into your dream.

As a kid I dreamed we'd got a new dog. He was a black labrador and I called him Prince. I was playing with him in the backyard and he started barking. I kept on hearing the barks. Finally, the barks woke me up and I realised I wasn't dreaming the barks, they were real. I went outside and found Dad in the backyard with a new black labrador pup.

Immobilising Dream

You can experience the feeling of being immobilised when something has awoken you before your astral body was ready to return. You haven't reintegrated back into your body properly and this splits your consciousness. You're awake and aware but you've got no control over your body because it's still asleep.

Nightmares

A nightmare is a fear that has been blown out of proportion that's playing out in your dream. If Suzie is playing with flowers in the garden and her mother screams out, 'Don't touch, there's a red-back spider,' later Suzie might dream about being chased by a gigantic hairy monster in the garden.

Lucid dreams

The most brilliant dreams are the ones when you realise you are having a dream while you are actually dreaming. This kind of dream lets you call the shots—where is it that you want to go, what would you like to do?

My nephew Daniel decided to find out what it would be like to control a dream.

'I wanted to fly, to feel free like a bird. Every night for a week I thought about flying. I'd say to myself, "I'm going to fly tonight," and it happened. It was incredible! I was dreaming and I knew it. I was flying through the air and saying to myself, "Now I want to fly over the ocean," and in seconds I was. I had flying dreams for the whole seven nights!'

Dreams are an important part of your spiritual make-up. If you use your sixth sense to analyse your dreams you'll gain valuable insight into life's little mysteries.

32

A Sixth Sense of Humour

From time to time you'll have a dream that will make you stand up and pay attention. Don't you find that every time you awaken to a deep realisation within yourself it feels like a magnificent sunrise? It really does make you wonder why you lingered so long in the blanket of night hiding from your true potential.

I spent most of my youth trying to convince myself that only special people were psychic, not 'normal' people like you or me. If I got an intuitive impression about something and it turned out to be right, as often it was, I didn't associate it with me being psychic. I didn't know why I knew things about the future, I just did. That was, until Upstairs (my guides) conspired to change my way of thinking. Their ammunition? Why, dangling the proverbial carrot at me! Only this carrot happened to have lotto numbers written all over it.

At the time this happened I was squandering my life working in a dead-end job at a newspaper. I hated my tele marketing role, and my drab work environment was whittling away at my passion until I felt almost completely eroded. Then one day I had an insight as I stared up from the computer. I realised I could end up here for the rest of my life. I looked around at the familiar faces of my co-workers and sighed. There was no trace of passion in their eyes. Some had been in the tele-sales department doing the same job for over twenty-five years. I could see myself at age sixty sitting in the same chair in front of the same computer, covered in cobwebs.

So what did I do about my situation? I started daydreaming about winning the lotto and how I would use my millions to escape to some wonderful tropical island. Pina colada in hand, lazing on a deckchair under a coconut tree, crystal clear blue seas—my dream lay in a bunch of numbers. I'd daydream about winning the lotto on the way to work, and while standing on the crowded train on cold winter evenings on my way home. As the months passed, I remained none the richer until one night I hit the jackpot. I had won the lotto! At least until I woke up to the deflating reality that it was only a dream. Then I realised I could remember four of the six numbers. Feeling this was a sign, I stopped by the newsagency in the morning and played those numbers though I still had to pick the other two at random. And guess what, the four numbers I dreamed of were drawn that night.

Encouraged by this amazing occurrence, I started focusing on lotto numbers, especially before going to sleep on Sunday nights (the night before the lotto draw). I kept saying, 'Ok, I'm going to see all six numbers in my dream tonight,' and like clockwork as each Sunday night rolled around, I'd dream about lotto numbers. Unfortunately, in the morning I could only ever remember four.

Much to my surprise, my four numbers were drawn each week but I never managed to guess the missing two that would have won me millions. This routine continued for over six months and it piqued others' interest. Eventually everyone at work was playing my numbers. They'd run up to me on Monday morning and say, 'Hey, Sue, what are the numbers?' before heading off in their lunch hour to play lotto based purely on what I'd seen in my dream. I realised they must have thought I was psychic and then it dawned on me—maybe I was.

That was when my lotto dreams stopped. Spirit managed to reel me in hook, line and sinker with that one realisation. Yes, those guys upstairs have a sixth sense of humour!

The universe gives you a helping hand to get you to where you're meant to be by putting little signposts on your road. Isn't it nice to know you're not on the road alone? Spirit guides you and gives you a boost when you need it. But you've still got to do some of the work; you can't expect them to do everything. You have the sixth sense. It's your gift. Why not use it? You can start by telling yourself, 'Yes, I do have the sixth sense'—and mean it. If you don't believe in your ability you've already set yourself up for failure.

The next step is to exercise your sixth sense. Practise sensing things. Start with simple tasks such as tuning in before you next open your email or Facebook, to see if you see in your mind's eye, or feel, who has sent you a message. Or when you next see a friend, tune into their energy and see if you pick up how they are feeling, or what's been happening in their life. The universe will give you the signs you need to keep you on your journey in life.

33

The Witching Hour

I know my guides don't like keeping regular office hours, how about yours? Why is it that paranormal activity always seems to happen at night?

Most people who share their experiences with me want to know why Spirit seems to let loose during the witching hour. Trust me; they don't have a cosmic curfew! Those who choose to visit can come and go as they please, and lost souls are pretty much stuck in this realm 24/7, so they're hanging around all the time. There's nothing magical or mystical about the night; the simple truth is that we're less distracted at night, especially in the quiet time before we drift off to sleep, so it's easier for them to get our attention. We're often so distracted during the day that we don't have time for ourselves let alone for our Spirit visitors to get a word in. Plus, we tend to be much more receptive once our conscious mind has gone into lock down and the intuitive mind has more breathing space.

When Tristan was eighteen he woke up in the middle of the night to the sound of voices and loud knocking on his bedroom window. He thought some of his friends were outside his bedroom so he got up and looked out the window. Nothing. He returned to bed and a few minutes later became terrified at the sight of three translucent beings standing at the foot of his bed.

'We have a job for you,' one of them told him telepathically. Too mortified to move, he could do nothing but listen. 'You are going to learn how to heal and protect people.' Then things got really strange and beams of bright light started emanating from their palms. This energy beamed straight into Tristan's hands.

'It's kind of like they had light sabres like you see in *Star Wars*,' he told me. 'I just watched the light for a while but then it got too freaky so I told them to go away.'

'Did they?' I asked.

'Yes, straight away,' he replied. 'Who were they?'

'Your guides.'

'How do you know?'

'The energy felt okay didn't it? It was strange because you're not used to it but it wasn't heavy, negative energy, was it?'

Then there are those visitors who we stumble across unexpectedly at night and the tables are turned and we're the intruder!

When my sister Frances was about eight years old she encountered an unexpected visitor after waking up from a bad dream. Not wanting to stay alone she decided to jump out of bed and go and spend the rest of the night with our mum. As the door to Mum's room creaked open, Frances saw a man who was surrounded by the most beautiful white light, stroking Mum's arm while she slept. Frances watched curiously as the man continued caressing Mum and then she noticed a gold signet ring set with a square gemstone on his little finger. Suddenly, the ethereal visitor stopped and looked up at my sister, smiled warmly and waved at her before disappearing.

The next day Frances told Mum about this visitor and described him. But it was when she mentioned the signet ring that tears welled up in Mum's eyes. She got up and took a photo out of the letter she received from Canada the previous day. Frances and I had only met our grandfather once when we were both under the age of five. The photo Mum showed us of him had been taken when he was lying in his coffin at the church before his burial, and there on his little finger was the exact same ring Frances had seen on the Spirit in Mum's room.

It's so comforting to know our loved ones keep the bonds between us, even from the other side. And I'm sure you'd love to have such a breathtaking experience yourself. What a pity our physical world demands most of our attention during the day that we can't pay attention to our Spirit visitors. Unless we set some quite time aside to tune in to them, they really don't have any other option but to call out to us in the middle of the night.

So if your bedroom is starting to look as busy as grand central station it's only because Spirit can't get your attention during the day. Honestly, they don't come out during the witching hour to scare us—they just want to let us know that they love and care about us enough to visit.

34

When to go Pro

Just when you think you've finally found your comfort zone, life has to mess things up by tossing you a jack-in-the-box surprise. In an unguarded moment you find yourself cornered by some unfathomable presence . . . and you're home alone. It's the first time something like this has happened and you're unprepared. What do you do if things get even stranger and objects start flying across the room? Do you stand there and pray it will go away? What if your prayers don't work immediately? It's 2 am, you don't have a car. You can grab your phone and run, but to where?

We all need a little help when the going gets rough. If you find yourself in the middle of a maelstrom, don't despair. Help is never too far away. Don't let uncertainty or pride get in the way. If you need help, then ask for it. Call a professional.

My students and I were called in to help eight-year-old Bella who was seeing an armless man in her room at night.

My student Mary recalls, 'Sue took us to do some "ghost busting". When we arrived Sue taught us how to section off parts of the house and check to see if we felt any presences.

'When we came to the laundry, which was next to a bedroom, I started to feel nauseous in the stomach. Sue asked to me to go to another part of the house and start clearing my chakras to see if this would make a difference. I did and the feelings ceased. As soon as I approached the laundry I started feeling sick again and could sense a presence there. When we entered the adjoining bedroom the presence was a lot stronger. I also picked up that the presence was of an older lady.

'I told Sue of these feelings and when Sue spoke to Bella the little girl informed us she spent a lot of time in that room and her grandmother (who had passed) came and visited her there often and she spoke with her. We discovered that the grandmother had stomach problems. No wonder I was feeling ill. I was rather pleased with myself for being able to pick up this energy and enjoyed being able to. We also discovered that the armless man was her uncle George who was checking in on her. This was a relief to everyone but the family asked why he appeared with no arms. Sue tuned in and said, "It's to help us identify his personality. He was a quiet man, someone who never reached out for what he wanted." They agreed. Even though their visitors ended up being family in Spirit, they were happy they had called us in as it put their minds at ease.'

It's comforting to know that there are professionals out there who are skilled in the art of dealing with paranormal activity. They don't scare easily, and armed with the right knowledge, they'll remove any invasive energy with minimal fuss. A good parapsychologist will also give you information about your paranormal event—what it is, why it happened and what you need to learn from it. By the time they leave your home will feel clear, calm and comfortable again.

So where do you find a professional parapsychologist when you need one? Unlike medicine, dentistry, mainstream psychotherapy and naturopathy, the parapsychology field is still largely unregulated and practitioners may not be classified in your local phone directory. If you have a real emergency and no idea where to turn, the first step might be to call a college that specialises in metaphysics. There's usually a parapsychologist on staff and if they can't help you they'll have excellent contacts to point you in the right direction.

You can call a psychic hotline to at least get a lead to a parapsychologist in your local area. As hotline practitioners generally have to meet certain qualifying standards and maintain a code of practice, their referrals are likely to reflect the same degree of ethics. New age shops also often give referrals, so why not pop in and ask at the counter? They usually know someone who can help. The classifieds section of new age magazines also carry listings of alternative practitioners.

But there are charlatans out there and it's always wise to trust in what your intuition tells you and keep a few things in mind. If you don't know what to look for in a professional here's a quick check list:

- What qualifications do they have?
- Ask them questions to gauge their level of understanding of paranormal activity. A good practitioner will be more than happy to spend time talking to you about what they know.
- Ask them for some tools or techniques you can use until they can visit in person.

- Make sure they're charging reasonable fees (that is, no more than the going hourly rate charged by any other therapist).
- Use your sixth sense—does this person *feel* right for you?
- Trust in your intuition and follow it.

Life isn't always clear cut. A sprinkling of the strange and bizarre helps us awaken to the realisation that our world has a lot of hidden secrets. Turning a blind eye from paranormal activity isn't going to make things disappear, taking definitive action gets better results. Supernatural forces can be dealt with. Empower yourself by either seeking a teacher who can help you gain the knowledge and skills you need to deal with these situations, or call in the experts.

35

Be Honest. Am I Totally Nuts?

Seeing strange lights, sensing spirits, talking to dead people . . . it's enough to make you wonder if you've gone totally nuts. But have you? Questioning your reality is natural part of being human. Somewhere along the path we all stumble onto something that makes us question what's real and wonder whether we're losing the plot. It might be a crisis or a lovely peak experience. Whatever it is, it makes you question your objective state of awareness. I think it's a positive thing because life shouldn't be about holding on to one truth. Instead, it should be a series of stepping stones leading you from personal childhood truths to an ultimate universal truth.

I remember the day when one of my childhood truths came crashing down. I was nine years old. It was Christmas Eve and my siblings and I were playing in the backyard when my big brother came running out of the house.

'You're not going to believe this,' he said. 'Santa is dead.'

I went numb at the news. 'What?'

I loved Christmas. Christmas Eve was the most magical night of the whole year. Nothing warmed my heart more than watching the lights playing off the beautiful glass baubles while I waited for Santa.

I ran inside. 'Mum, is Santa really dead?' I demanded.

She was silent for a moment too long. 'Don't get upset,' she said. 'Santa isn't real.'

The bombshell went straight to my heart and cracked the magic of Christmas forever. Now I make it my mission to find the truth and to openly embrace new realities. This means I'm smashing outdated beliefs every time I venture into the unknown.

Kids have a wonderful imagination so it's easy to discount things they say, especially when it doesn't fit in with your take on reality.

'When Annalysse was four she started seeing the reflection of her grandmother in the wardrobe mirror. We had a beautiful antique wardrobe with a mirror flanked on both sides by lovely walnut timber. Annalysse kept telling us that there was a lady in the mirror,' said Mel. 'At first we didn't know what to think. Was it her imagination? But the weeks passed and she was still talking about the woman she could see. One night we asked her older sister to sleep in Annalysse's room to see if anything unusual happened. She came running out and told us she saw the old lady in the mirror. I decided to move the bed to face away from the mirror and hoped this would put an end to things,' said Mel, her face animated as she recounted the story.

'We had inherited the wardrobe from my husband's grandparents and decided to put it in Annalysse's room. Shortly after she started to see the mysterious woman in the mirror. One day I was telling my husband's sister the story about the old lady. Annalysse had described her as having black stockings, frilly clothes and blonde hair with really big curls and blue eyes.'

Mel started smiling. 'His sister said, "Oh, that's Nan. That's what she used to look like back in the early days, around about the time when she bought the wardrobe. She loved it.'

Mel had never met David's grandmother and there were no pictures of her as a younger woman in the house to influence little Annalysse, but now Mel knew who the lady in the mirror was.

There's a fine line between reality and illusion. Working in metaphysics sometimes makes you wonder if you're a reality fringe dweller. Being confronted by discarnate beings, looking into the future, healing people with energy coming out of your hands—some people think all this is nuts. The fact that I do this kind of stuff for a living seems even more questionable to them. But just because I work with a different understanding of reality doesn't mean I'm certifiable. I'm actually pretty grounded because I trust my intuition, and blend science and common sense together with Spirit. So, while I don't anticipate any trips to the funny farm, I still appreciate that much of our reality is subjective. This is what makes us truly unique—we see things through different eyes.

36

Be Home by Midnight

Once I decided it was time to make friends with my sixth sense, I enrolled to do a course in metaphysics, which is all about personal, psychic and spiritual development. I became acquainted with terms such as clairvoyance, clairaudience and clairsentience. I hadn't realised there were so many different types of psychic faculties, with mediumship and telepathy being only the start. I also discovered the realm of Spirit which included angels, Spirit guides and assorted astral beings.

The biggest gift I got from studying metaphysics was the wisdom that comes from understanding other realms of reality and the invaluable knowledge that the universe never sends us a challenge we can't overcome. After that first ghost in my house, I would jump at the slightest sound in the middle of the night, and look at me now—I even take some of my students on ghost busts! As I am writing this book I'm working on a television series about ghost stories and I'll be venturing up to a 'haunted' old gaol to film an overnight stay in the notorious 'room' where angels fear to tread. Due to my experience, at times I forget how overwhelming these types of encounters can be for people.

I'll never forget the metaphysics retreat I ran a few years ago in Stroud, a small country town north of Newcastle. A storm was brewing as we drove down the country road and into the driveway of the old mud-brick monastery, now a country retreat. It used to be run by the nuns of the Order of Chiara and since both my college and my daughter are called Chiara I was drawn to this place, and also because of its promise of rustic tranquillity.

The storm intensified as the students and I gathered in the common room to discuss the activities for the weekend. As the thunder clapped (clichéd I know) I looked at an old turntable and to my amusement noticed the soundtrack from *Ghostbusters* sitting on it. Just then two students came running in claiming that their bedroom door had jammed all by itself and they were sure there was a ghost. They seemed a little startled when I cheerfully assured them that there was more than one ghost here, but one of my male students—I'll call him Joe—was unperturbed, 'Bring it on. Let the ghost come and get me tonight.'

We all retired late and in the morning there was some commotion in the breakfast room. Some students were excited, others a little unsettled.

'Did you hear what happened to the boys last night?' quizzed one of the girls. 'The ghost of a woman appeared in Joe's room and scared him so he ran into Travis' room. It followed him in and then they both got frightened and ran into the living room.'

I turned to Travis, 'And then what did you do? Did you clear the ghost?'

'God, no!' he said. 'We just slammed the door shut and huddled together on the lounge hoping it would go away!'

I couldn't help myself and started laughing, which is the last thing a teacher should do. I looked at both of them and said, 'So, if it could get into your bedroom, why couldn't it get into the living room?'

They both looked totally surprised. 'That's right,' I said. 'It could have come for you there but it didn't. Do you know why? Because you felt safe and protected in the living room.'

What the boys should have done was to stand their ground and ask the ghost to leave them. Sometimes that's all it takes—a simple command. This doesn't work on all ghosts, but it works on a lot of them. Another method is to invoke a simple prayer or mantra like, 'In the name of God (or whatever other deity you relate to), I ask that Spirit clear this lost soul for me.'

I love the power of the mind!

37

Chain-rattlers Anonymous

Not everything that goes bump in the night is a chain-rattling ghost or malevolent demon. Sometimes people can misinterpret what they see and feel.

When Ashleigh called me to check out her elderly aunt's 'haunted house,' I chose to bring several students with me to give them a first-hand experience of what a ghost feels like and how to remove it if necessary.

When we entered the house we were immediately greeted by a heavy, thick atmosphere laden with fear. Some of the students reacted to this energy, saying there had to be a really negative Spirit lurking there.

'Are you sure?' I asked. 'Tune in again. Is the heaviness coming from a conscious life form? Or is it a projection of energy? Feel it.'

This time a few of them remarked that it was the energy of the room, not of a lost soul. Bingo! They had recognised that there was a difference in energy. You can pick up these subtleties if you pay attention. There wasn't a dark menacing ghost rampaging around the place, the energy came from Ashleigh's own fear. She was constantly worrying that there was something haunting her and had created the heavy atmosphere.

I sat Ashleigh down and gently told her this. 'But,' she said disillusioned, 'there's something in my house, I know it. I can feel it.'

'Yes, but it's not what you think,' I tried to reassure her. 'You've been praying a lot for your husband to visit you, haven't you?'

Tears welled in her eyes, 'Yes, every day since he died, for the last six months, but he never visits me. I can't believe he doesn't care enough about me to visit!'

'He is here. He's been here every day, he sits with you at night while you watch television. Surely you've felt him do that?'

She had, but thought it was her imagination because she wanted him to be with her so badly.

She couldn't understand why the room felt so heavy if her husband was present. I very tactfully explained that the heaviness was her creation—a mix of her fear, grief and feelings of abandonment. Her loving husband was indeed visiting her.

She was overwhelmed. 'Really?' she cried. 'He's keeping me company?'

She lightened up immediately. It made a world of difference to know she wasn't alone at night, that her husband was keeping a watchful eye over her.

•

I remember the first time I discovered that there are some really lovely ghosts out there. I went to have a psychic reading with an old Indian man in a beachside town soon after my own ghostly ordeals. After having a ghost in my house, and encountering an army of ghosts in Ios, I firmly believed all ghosts were something to be frightened of. The reader was still in a session with a client when I arrived and he asked me to wait in the living room. It was a lovely, comfortable room warmed by the glow of flames licking the tinder in the fireplace. I leaned back on the lounge and relaxed, feeling very much at home.

'Hello, dear.'

The voice came out of thin air. I slowly turned my head towards my left shoulder and saw a little old lady sitting next to me knitting. I shook my head and looked again, but she was still there.

'It's nice with the fire on, isn't it?' she said, a huge smile lighting up her pleasant face.

I backed into the lounge and crossed my arms, half expecting her to morph from a beautiful little granny into some nightmarish ghoul.

Halfway through my reading I mustered up the courage to ask, 'Is it my imagination or is there a ghost in your living room?' I awaited his ridicule.

'Oh, you mean the little old lady?' he smiled.

'Er, the one knitting.'

'Yes, that's her. Isn't she lovely?'

I raised an eyebrow, 'But she's dead!'

He grinned and looked at me with thoughtful eyes. 'Do you think that all ghosts really walk around dragging chains? Some are happy being here. She's earthbound but she loves being here because she's not in any kind of trauma. This place was her home and she couldn't part from it when she died, so she chose to remain here. It doesn't bother me and I like her company. Why should I kick her out?'

I know it might sound a little crazy at times thinking that your place is an open house to all sorts of spirits. But I think it's kind of nice knowing that our friends and family who have passed over are constantly popping in to visit. Even when I meet a lovely Spirit that isn't related to me I know there's always a reason for it, something I need to learn from my encounter.

I know some people become uncomfortable when you tell them Spirit is always popping in and out. Let me assure you they respect your privacy. They know when to turn the other way!

If you stay open to the adventure of life you find it is much easier to embrace Spirit at your own pace. After a little while you'll discover that it is easy to let go of apprehension and uncertainty. Before you know it you'll be chatting to them like old friends.

38

When Dad Came to Visit

I've since learned that there really isn't a reason to kick out most spirits. Obviously you want to clear out lost souls who are experiencing trauma—they're more than happy being rescued and sent home. And no one wants uninvited malevolent beings hanging around—they have no right being in your home. But, have you ever thought about the idea that you might be the one inviting in some of these spirits? Sometimes we inadvertently invite in spirits by thinking about them and get caught off guard when they do appear.

When my dad died from cancer on All Saints' Day in 2001, the last thing Mum expected was a midnight call from his Spirit. But, three weeks later, he did just that. He timed his visit well. It was the first night Mum was on her own after having my sisters and I spending nights with her.

Because it was a warm November night Mum only had a cotton sheet over her as she lay in bed in the changeover period between being awake and asleep. Suddenly the sheet went flying off her, down past her feet and fell to the floor. Mum panicked. She didn't know what kind of invisible force it was but she intuitively cried out, 'Michael, leave me alone!'

She didn't know what to do. In the dark of night everything seems a little more overwhelming than it does in the light of day. Too scared to go to sleep, she spent the rest of the night in apprehension of another strike.

The next day Mum caught up with Chichina, my dad's cousin, who was married to his best friend Carlo. Carlo died exactly six weeks before Dad, and both Mum and Chichina took comfort in knowing their husbands were in heaven together, hanging out just as they had in life. Mum told Chichina about Dad's visit and how he swept the sheet off her and onto the floor.

'No,' said Chichina. 'You don't say. Carlo did the same thing to me a few weeks ago. It scared the hell out of me.'

When Mum told me about her harrowing event she asked me why both Carlo and Dad would do this to their wives.

I replied, 'Because they've got a good sense of humour? They wanted to get your attention.'

'Couldn't they have done it in a nicer way?'

I smiled. 'They weren't trying to scare the pair of you. But you have been thinking about them, missing them and wishing they were here, right? So, they thought this stunt would give you proof that they were alive and well in Spirit. Look how they co-ordinated the event, both leaving the same calling card—tossing the bed covers onto the floor. It's their way of showing they still care about you both.'

What a unique way of calling to say 'I love you!'

Here's something you can do to work with the dearly departed: ask them to give you a calling card, one you'd be comfortable with. Dad's calling card scared Mum, you don't want the same thing happening to you. So, think about what would work for you. Some people ask for their loved one to sit on their bed and stroke their arm, others prefer the scent of perfume, others will ask for a light to switch on. Once you have your preferred calling card in place, you'll feel comfortable when it's activated. It'll confirm they are actually in the room with you. Then you can start talking to them.

There will be times when strange things happen around the house. Before you jump to conclusions, tune in and see what's really behind it.

I remember one night when I was home alone. Around 2 am the bedroom door, which was wide open, slammed shut. It was so loud it made me jump. I got up and checked the hall for a draught. Then I checked the bedroom windows. The air was perfectly still. I sat on the corner of my bed and tuned in to find out what was going on. The last thing I needed at that time of the morning was to have a disruptive entity invading my space, especially when I was home alone. I discovered it was my father paying me a visit. He thought slamming the door shut would get my attention. Great!

I wasn't scared when the door slammed. That's the benefit of working with my sixth sense; it gives me a sense of calm that helps me gain control over daunting situations. Unlike my mother who was scared by Dad's shenanigans, I jumped back into bed and asked him to telepathically communicate with me. It was the perfect time to catch up and see how things were going. After all, I put out an open invitation to his soul to visit me whenever he wants, so he does!

I consider moments like this to be a true blessing. You will too the moment you let go of fear and learn to trust in your sixth sense.

39

My Bags are Packed, I'm Ready

Knowing what to expect of death can really make a difference in how well you handle the journey. Death can be a profoundly liberating experience if you can move out of fear or denial. Why fret away your precious last months, weeks, days or hours of life fighting destiny?

Attitudes to death vary from culture to culture and this influences people's perception of death. And perception is what makes the difference. Even after someone has passed on, our attitudes to death influence how we cope with our loss. Having worked with my sixth sense for over twenty years I know what to expect from death. I know what's waiting for us and I can tell you it is beautiful. How different life would be if every person on the planet knew this.

Death is a part of a natural cycle that heralds the end of one life on earth and the beginning of another in the Spirit world. One lifetime here is a drop in the immortal ocean of the soul. At death the soul returns home to the Spirit world where it continues living and learning. Knowing this helps lots of people bear the pain of separation and accept death.

I'd like to share an experience I had recently. I've changed the names for the family's sake.

It was 5 pm and I was sitting in the ICU waiting room with my spiritual healing student, Isabella. It was my fourth visit to see thirty-four-year-old Paul, who was in a coma after a brain tumour operation. The doctors couldn't get him out. The family was desperate and asked me to help. But spiritual healers are usually the last wild card in these kinds of scenarios and the family found our presence unsettling.

The patient responded well to our energy work. He was always more active when we were working on him. He even clenched his fist in response once or twice, which made his wife's eyes light up. She was so brave. She had lost her dad to a brain haemorrhage a few weeks earlier, and had a one-year-old child and was spending all her days and nights at the hospital desperately trying to help her man wake up. Every little movement he made inspired her, every set back pushed her to the brink of despair.

I tuned in. The first time I saw Paul in hospital, Isabella and I tuned in and we felt his Spirit. He had a lovely and happy energy. His Spirit told us that he loved McDonalds and soccer. It was a message from limbo. His wife smiled, 'Yes, he loves them both.' Despite being able to talk with his Spirit, we couldn't get Paul out of his coma.

I talked to Paul's soul and a Spirit butted in. 'It's Joanna. I'm his nanna.' We told his wife and she replied that wasn't his nanna's name. But Joanna wouldn't leave me alone. She was persistent. She was there looking after him. He was in safe hands.

Outside in the waiting room eager relatives greeted me. I told them Joanna was looking after him. His aunt smiled at me, 'That's *our* nanna.' His father nodded in confirmation.

Paul's mother burst into tears. 'She's not coming to take him away, is she?'

My brief before I saw Paul was to give them no bad news. I tell them she's just looking after him. But Paul is in a coma, and time is running out.

The next time I saw Paul, his energy was low, too low. Unlike on previous visits, when he could hold his own and it was easy to talk to his soul, his energy had dissipated. It was not a good sign. But, the thing was, we were still able to pass messages from him to his family and we were talking to his relatives on the other side. Most coma patients linger in silence, Paul was lucky.

On my next visit Paul had a fever. He couldn't connect with his body. I knew this would be my last visit. A few nights earlier I dreamed I was at the hospital and my guides told me this was my last shot—that Paul's prognosis was really bad. He was not responsive; his body was just too tired. Three weeks later he died.

Confronting death on a daily basis was emotionally exhausting for the family, especially because they didn't know much about what happens when you die. The fact that Paul was aware of us while in a coma and that there were relatives like Joanna around didn't soothe their pain or make it any easier. Death was so final in their eyes. They wanted Paul out of the coma and smiling again. They wanted him back in their lives.

Death is such a sensitive topic and I appreciate and respect that we all see it through different eyes. I hope that by letting you know that Spirit is always with you and that you never die alone is comforting. Know that your soul is immortal and that when you die you move on to the next stage in an incredible journey.

40

On the Edge of Forever

Some people are privileged enough to witness the soul lifting up from the body after being liberated by death. They describe it as being one of the most incredible moments in their lives. This magnificent and awe-inspiring moment is full of peace and they can see and feel the serenity of the departing soul. Its lightness of being filters through and it emanates unconditional love. They sense that the person is ok, that death is ok and there really isn't anything to fear. Knowing this makes letting go so much easier.

Because most people are so full of sadness when their loved one is dying they end up blocking their sixth sense and missing this aspect of the souls' transition. Instead they get caught up in wondering whether or not there's life after death, or if the soul is going to get lost in some strange realm or end up earthbound wandering the world in search of peace. Death strikes fear in most of us because we don't really know what's going to happen while we're dying nor what happens after we're dead. I want to shed some light on this so you can release any fears you might have.

The death process starts about three months before you die when the death mantle encases your soul. The death mantle is energy activated by your soul. It is in keeping with your soul's blueprint which determines when you die. Once it covers your soul it starts reducing the inflow of universal and earth energy. Your soul is slowly depleted of its essential nutrients. Then, three days prior to death, the seven main chakras begin shutting down, and the earth star and transpersonal point, centres that anchor you in the physical reality, slowly open up in preparation for the soul's journey back home. And then you die.

Some would say: that's it, you've pulled up stumps and there's nothing more. I know that death is only the beginning of the next leg of your amazing journey—the journey back home to the Spirit world. I know that once there you spend time being healed and 'debriefed' on your former life and are free to do what you want. You could choose to be a Spirit guide and look after family and friends, or simply enjoy 'being'. Life in the Spirit realm isn't like our nine-to-five lives here. You can manifest whatever you want and even visit countless different realms. The edge of forever is a wonderful place to park your soul. You are eternal.

•

When my uncle Frank was asleep in bed in the cancer ward, a specialist came to check on him late on a Friday afternoon. He conducted an examination and told my aunt that Frank was stable and he would review his status on the Monday morning. Not long after this I asked Stephen, my husband at the time, who was an intuitive spiritual healer, to check in on my uncle. I asked him to check Uncle Frank's earth star and chakras and to check out the hospital room for relatives in Spirit. It was my way of finding out how much time he had left.

Stephen noticed all of Uncle Frank's chakras were low on energy and starting to shut down and that his earth star—one of his centres—was wide open, all clear signs that the death process had begun. He also saw the Spirit of my grandmother in the room hovering around my uncle. Our relatives in Spirit do that before we die. They pop into our room and keep a vigil over us and are there to hold our hand as we walk up the tunnel of light across to the other side. When he told me this I immediately called up my cousin Roy and told him to call his three brothers to prepare them for the inevitable.

Roy said that the doctors had told his mother that his dad was stable and they were going to review him on the Monday. I said, 'He won't be alive by Monday morning. Listen, Roy, your brother is interstate, why don't you call him and ask him to fly up. I honestly believe your dad won't last till Monday morning despite what the doctors are telling you.'

He did what I asked him to do. Late on the Sunday night I was half asleep in bed when I suddenly felt a million and one pins and needles throughout my body. It felt like my etheric body was lifting away from my physical one. I experienced this sensation for about twenty minutes before I finally managed to move and sit up in bed. Let me tell you, it was one of the strangest sensations I've ever experienced. I knew then that my uncle was definitely dying—I was feeling part of the process energetically because I had a close bond with him.

We got a call from Roy about six the next morning to say his dad had crossed over.

I was so glad to know my grandmother was there with him when he died and I was relieved to know the family all got together to see him before he left. That's one of the beautiful things about working with the sixth sense; it really does help you help others.

41

When it's Someone Else's Stuff

One beautiful aspect of the soul is that a small amount of our energy can speak volumes. You don't have to say a word to get a message across as others can sense what you're thinking and feeling because your energy says it all.

You have a unique energetic signature that sets you apart from everything else. It's a wonderful blend of your thoughts, feelings, personal history and soul-essence all wrapped up into a lovely package. This package has a boundary—a natural field that acts as a buffer zone between you and the world. It gives you definition, a clear sense of what is yours and what is not.

Occasionally your boundary is compromised and you end up being affected by other people's energy. Without realising it, you've taken on someone else's stuff. There are a few reasons why this happens. Sometimes illness can lower your energy making it easier to enmesh with others. The process is like osmosis—another person's feelings filter into your spiritual membrane because your own boundary can't shield you well enough. Sometimes it's one-sided and you end up being on the receiving end of thoughts and feelings that aren't yours, but you think they are because you can't discern the difference. Other times you know they're not yours but it surprises you because you can actually feel it!

Sherry told me her story.

'A couple of months ago one of the supervisors at work was acting strangely and as I had recently starting using it again, my boss asked me if I could "see" what was wrong with her as he knew I had some ability. Because I hadn't tried it for twenty years, I didn't think I would be able to, but straight away I saw a murky energy around this supervisor's chest. The next day she announced she had breast cancer. I felt dreadful, as if I had invaded her privacy. I'm not sure if something like that is an unethical thing to do—to read people when they haven't given you permission. In any event, my experience of physically feeling this woman's back and breathing problems was kind of thrust upon me and I didn't ask for it. I have since cut the cords from her and I am starting to feel better.'

When there's any kind of energy exchange between people it's easy to be affected by the other person's stuff. It's possible even when standing next to someone on a crowded train to unwittingly take on board their mood. This happens because you're energy fields become entangled. Thankfully this kind of energy exchange is usually short lived; it won't linger on for days or weeks.

There can be positive outcomes as well. Your boundary automatically drops when you open up to someone. Feelings of love, compassion and empathy open your energies and this creates a doorway for an energetic transfer of thoughts and feelings between the two of you. Often this creates a mutual exchange of energies which gives you that feel-good factor.

Let's explore the other types of energy exchange that can affect you. One type is called a cord. If you're constantly thinking about someone, your energy actively creates an energetic cord that reaches out and connects the two of you. If the other person's open and reciprocates your energy then you have a mutual cord. Love is the energy that's usually behind mutual cords, and you don't find many people complaining about this!

Have you ever been so in love, that it feels as if you've merged into your partner? I can tell you there's more than one energetic cord binding you together. We call it field entanglement. And I'm sure you wouldn't want to have it any other way. This deep connection literally sends you into the stratosphere. A nuclear bomb could go off in the backyard and you would barely notice. The world's a beautiful place when you've got this connection going. But when the energy cords between you break—if, for example, one of you wants to end things—you'll feel the separation at a deep energetic level. A part of you has literally been severed because the cords have been cut.

When a relationship breaks down it can create another energetic state called a hook. This can happen if you want to move on with your life, but your partner doesn't want to let go of you. Simply by being reluctant to let go, they can end up creating hooks that attach to your energy and this keeps the link alive. Most people do this unintentionally. They have no idea they've created an energetic hook. But they have because they can't stop thinking about you; they still love you and want to stay connected. When an energy is one-sided, and it stems from lower vibration emotions such as grief, fear, anger or pain, it creates this invasive type of energy.

Another invasive energy is an attachment, or a projection of a negative thought form. It is also referred to as a phantom energy. A phantom energy doesn't have consciousness or its own life force. It is created by repetitive thinking so amplifies the one thought. You don't need to be standing next to, or even know the person, to be affected by this kind of energy. If someone repeatedly and intensely sends you a negative thought form such as, 'I hope you lose your job!', unless you have strong boundaries, it can get embedded in your energy field.

The phantom energy creates an attachment which blocks the flow of your own energy. It's not uncommon to find these attachments around your head or shoulder area, but they can also be found near your other chakras as well. This energy acts like a magnet and, since like attracts like, a negative energy can come back to you. Within a short period of time you might start experiencing problems with your boss and even end up losing your job. This isn't fair because someone else sent it to you, but I am letting you know that this kind of thing can happen.

Being on the receiving end of lower vibrations through hooks, attachments and phantom energies is the uglier side of taking on someone else's stuff. But there are many projections that can channel lovely energies to you. Linking with other people's energies can create a sense of euphoria and love, and we can all use a good dose of that. Think about your own experiences like when you fell in love, or how you formed a new close friendship. Can you remember the kind of energy, or the feeling that encouraged you to form a closer bond with them?

You can't control what people think and feel, but you can choose what energies you want to hold on to. And this knowledge will empower you. Remember that energy isn't like a piece of elastic that can be stretched only so far then retract; it's non-linear and can transcend time and space.

Most people never complain about receiving people's energy when the essence is full of love. But if you feel your wellbeing is being affected because you've taken on someone else's stuff here's what you can do to clear it.

First, recognise the thought and feeling. Does it belong to you? Make a conscious decision to let go of anything that doesn't. Flush your entire soul with white light and you'll feel better in no time. If the thought or feeling lingers on for days, it's likely that it was yours to begin with. Spend a few minutes focusing on this unwanted energy. Ask your Spirit guides to show you what emotional or psychological issues you need to look at. They can give you helpful advice on how to deal with the issue and how to heal yourself. For example, they may tell you how to accept the issue, or whether you need to seek counselling or get some healing.

42

Finding the Right Way Home

When the energy you're feeling isn't your own, and it's not coming from someone next to you, it makes you wonder. If you look carefully you might discover that what you are picking up on are thoughts and feelings that belong to lost souls. Their thoughts and feelings are as real as your own because it's still energy, a vibe that you are picking up. Once you realise that this energy is coming from a lost soul, you can take control of the situation by helping them find the right way home.

'This is something I had to come to terms with,' said Tori. 'My partner Tim seemed to have a whole entourage of lost souls following him around. It's something I've had to adapt to. They follow me home and refuse to leave. One night I got up in the early hours to visit the bathroom. I didn't bother to switch on any lights as it was just a short walk across the hallway. On my way back across the hall, I was confronted by a dark shadow and, terrified, I began to scream. The shadow then started screaming . . . it turned out to be Tim and we'd frightened the living daylights out of each other! After cursing him for scaring me I asked him what he was playing at. He told me that he saw 'me' come back into the bedroom, felt the impression in the bed and the warmth of a body next to him, so figured the coast was clear and got out to use the bathroom himself.

'As it dawned on us that it must have been a Spirit that got cosy with Tim in bed, we went running into the bedroom to check it out, but there was nothing to be seen. We both slept a little uneasily that night.

'Nothing like that has happened since. But there was a spell a couple of months later when all the photographs in our bedroom kept getting turned to face the wall. We would turn them back to face the right way then leave the room and the next time we went back in they would be facing the wall again.

'Not long after that we had to move as our house was being sold. I secretly hoped that we would also make a clean break from the spirits. On our first day in our new place we were standing at one end of the kitchen unpacking boxes. I felt these thoughts and emotions around me and something brushed past me. Then, the washing-up liquid bottle started to tip backwards and forwards two or three times, then steadied itself. It was like we were being sent a message: "We're still here; we moved with you!"'

Tori knew she had a choice. She could continue living with these lost souls, constantly picking up on their energies, or she could send them home to the Spirit world.

Working with the sixth sense opens up many different paths. For some people the path leads to rescuing lost souls. You might think being a professional ghostbuster isn't your thing. But, just in case you find yourself face to face with a lost soul, it's better to be equipped with a little knowledge. Knowing how to handle any situation always gives you a sense of control. Being of service to lost souls is rewarding work.

I've found that most ghosts are beautiful souls. And why wouldn't they be? They're just like you and me minus a body. They have the same thoughts, feelings and issues they had when they were alive. The only difference is that you have the freedom to move on with your life, and they're stuck. This is where you can help. You can be their go-between, their link between heaven and earth.

Lost souls are not here to haunt or torment us. Most just want to get home to the Spirit world so they can start the next chapter in their life. But they don't know who to call on, or how to open a portal to the next world, because they have been separated from their higher self. A lost soul gets stuck in the lower consciousness and this means they're separated from the aspect of themselves that can get in touch with their guides and the Spirit world. They can only negotiate their experiences through the eyes of the ego, which is the lower self. It holds on to what it knows about its former physical life and this is the world the lost souls recreate in limbo. They continue experiencing this reality until they realise they are actually dead and call for help.

Sometimes help comes in the form of angels and Spirit guides. They create a tunnel of light which is a doorway home. This tunnel is full of the most enchanting energy to help entice the soul towards it. Words describing the luminous light and the energy of unconditional love that the tunnel holds cannot do justice. It is up to the lost soul to enter the light. Spirit cannot force them. Lost souls have free will, so Spirit can only offer assistance. Unfortunately some lost souls hesitate to move into the light despite seeing the Spirit helpers waiting for them. They're confused and don't necessarily understand that the Spirit helpers are benevolent beings, or they might feel undeserving and so they step back. Eventually the doorway to the Spirit world will close. But another can open at a later stage if the lost soul asks for help again.

Did you know that your prayers can help open a doorway for lost souls? Any thoughts you send out for the wellbeing of a departed one will help them, especially if they're earthbound. Your prayers indirectly invite guardian angels to step in and open a portal. Yes, prayer is powerful!

It's no coincidence if a lost soul finds its way to you. They might gravitate towards you because your higher self actually invites them over or it might be part of your destiny to overcome a fear of lost souls or to broaden your knowledge of spiritual beings. Sometimes a lost soul is drawn to you because *your* soul shines brightly. Perhaps they sense something in your energy that makes them feel safe and secure. Being of service to a lost soul is a wonderful spiritual experience; I certainly wouldn't turn one away. Remember how frightened I was of the first ghosts I encountered? And, now I'm happy to work with them.

Here is something you can do to help a lost soul cross over to the light:

> Call on the soul's guides to come to your assistance. Ask them to create a tunnel of light, or dimensional doorway, between here and the Spirit world and to bring along with them a family member so the lost soul will feel comfortable

enough to step into the light. Ask the guardians of light to reunite the lost soul with their family. Once the lost soul steps into the dimensional doorway you can ask for it to close. This seals off the link between the two worlds and you can get on with your day.

Some people go through life never seeing a lost soul. Others see them all the time. If you are born to be of service to a lost soul then one will meet you somewhere along the path. If you are lucky enough to find yourself in this situation try to step out of your comfort zone and help them. It can be an immensely rewarding experience. Tori is happy now that she has learned how to clear lost souls for herself. If you don't feel you're ready to take that step, then call in a professional.

If you fear encountering a lost soul, I want you to consider this. If you saw a child crying in a shopping centre because they'd lost their mother, you'd go over and help, wouldn't you? There's no difference between this and a lost soul crying for its home and friends. Both want to be with their familiar surroundings and loved ones. The only difference is that one has a body so it's easy to understand the world they live in; the other lives in an unfamiliar realm which might seem a little daunting until you shift your awareness. A soul is a soul, with or without a body.

43

They're Here . . .

There's a lot more going on in our world than most people realise. An unseen world is alive and well in different dimensional realities. Surreal, beautiful, enchanting, there are realms you'll simply love to connect with, especially the angelic realm. But, there are some realms, like the lower astral realm, that have disturbing energies. While most lost souls are relatively harmless, there are some angry souls, known as poltergeists, that linger in our world.

I'd like to share a story with you. Max, a journalist, called Stephen because he wanted to do an article on the paranormal. He asked if he could accompany Stephen on a ghost bust so that he could write the piece from first-hand experience. Stephen explained that unless you can see and feel energy, or unless there's a poltergeist in the house moving objects around, it was quite boring to watch a 'ghost bust'. But Max was still interested in watching Stephen work.

Three days after the phone call from Max, Stephen and I were listening to a news story about a poltergeist in a sleepy town near Darwin. The radio journalist reporting the story ran out of the house in fear. She talked about how the residents of the cottage were being assaulted by flying objects, watching rooms being trashed, dodging gravel coming down from the ceiling and finding messages printed in pebbles on their bathroom floor.

A day later Stephen was on a plane with Max and a sceptical television crew. Their brief was to expose this story as a hoax; however, if the story was true and they captured poltergeist activity on film, it would be a world exclusive.

After an uneventful day in the haunted house one of the cameramen called over Max and the producer to watch his camera switch on and off by itself. Their scepticism began evaporating as the cameraman said aloud, 'If you think you're so smart, turn the camera on,' and the poltergeist obliged—the presence started switching the camera on and off several times! Strangely, every time there was some ghostly action in the house the crew failed to capture it on film. The most frustrating incident occurred when they were all sitting in the kitchen and out of the blue a baby's bottle sitting on top of the microwave went flying across the room. Everyone watched in stunned silence that quickly turned to excitement because the camera should have caught it. When they viewed the film all they had captured was the leg of one of the crewmen walking in front of the camera at exactly the same moment the bottle was flying across the room. This was no stupid poltergeist.

Stephen spent several hours doing a clearance in the cottage and the poltergeist went away. The crew returned to Sydney and things were quiet for three days. Then the producer called to say that the lady of the house claimed the poltergeist was back. The only way an entity can ever return to this dimension is if it is invited back by the person it is connected to within the first three days of its removal. So we assumed she must have asked it back, but why?

The show went to air as a three-day exclusive program. On the third night, before they were due to screen an interview with Stephen, the producers received a segment of film rushed down from a reporter in Darwin who had been employed by the local court to find evidence of a 'presence' because the landlord of the house wanted to sue the residents for damage done to the premises. The film captured a shot of a golf ball flying across the living room. On closer examination there appeared to be a reflection in a glass wall unit of a woman throwing the ball. The station immediately killed the story, claiming the woman of the haunted house had set up the whole thing because she wanted people to believe her story. In the end she lost all credibility and the producer lost his job.

A week later Max called Stephen to say he'd spoken to the Darwin reporter and he claimed the reflection was a mystery because the woman was not even in the room when the incident occurred. Did she invite the poltergeist back because she wanted more people to believe her account of events? It was too late . . . the media had already killed the story.

If you feel there's a heavy and unsettling presence in your home, take action. I usually advise people to seek professional help when dealing with poltergeists. Professionals won't feel overwhelmed or intimidated by one and can usually have your place feeling clear and peaceful in no time at all.

People's attitudes to the paranormal are becoming more sophisticated. They're starting to awaken to their intuitive abilities and catch glimpses of lost souls and Spirit guides and incorporating these concepts into their everyday awareness. Collectively, we're moving to embrace new realities, so don't feel that there's something wrong with you, that you're delusional because you're starting to see strange things. The unseen world is slowly being revealed to us all.

44

Double Or Nothing

The paranormal world is full of so many astonishing things, it can be confusing to begin with. I'm sure that until you read about poltergeists, they seemed eerie and strange. Some of the mystique disappears once you discover what they really are and how you can help them return to the Spirit world. Another fascinating and strange phenomenon is the doppelganger.

A doppelganger is an 'energy' double, or look-alike, of a living person. They are not, as many people think, a carbon-copy of the physical you. Popular culture usually associates doppelgangers with sinister or evil things, seeing them as harbingers of bad luck. Some traditions hold the belief that if someone sees a doppelganger hanging around you it means you're going to get seriously ill, others believe that if you see your own doppelganger it's an omen you're going to die. Mary Shelley, the author of *Frankenstein*, reported in a letter to a friend that before her husband, poet Percy Bysshe Shelley, drowned, he'd told her he had met his doppelganger.

Is this ghostly double real? Could the doppelganger be a projection of your spiritual body preparing to leave a few days before you die? Is the doppelganger actually the death mantle? The death mantle is not a conscious energy because it doesn't have intelligence or awareness. It's an energy that has been created by the soul when it knows it's time for you to return home to Spirit. It's created about three months before death, in keeping with your karma which sets your biological clock before birth.

About three days before you die, your chakras slowly shut down in keeping with your soul's plan. This means you're not going to get enough life-force energy to keep your body going and in a few days you'll die. Some people see their doppelganger during this period. It's a way of preparing the person, giving them time to consciously accept what will happen to them.

'That makes sense if your soul creates it,' said Nikki in class one day. 'But what I'm worried about is, if you can create one through worrying about being sick?'

'Yes,' I replied, 'Because your thoughts create your reality.'

She shifted uncomfortably in her seat.

I smiled. 'But remember if you've created it then it is a phantom energy—a projection of your thoughts only. It doesn't have consciousness so you can dismantle it as easily as you created it.'

She felt better after hearing this. There's nothing worse than thinking you can't stop something negative once it has manifested.

Sometimes a curse can create a doppelganger-like energy around people and make them ill.

'The doctors can't find anything wrong with her,' explained Belinda's mother as I sat by Belinda's beside. 'But look at her, she can't move. I know there's something wrong. I feel it. I sense some kind of interference.' Belinda's mother trusted her sixth sense.

'Could it be a doppelganger?' she asked. 'Because that's the image I keep getting when I close my eyes and tune in.'

I carefully scanned Belinda's aura and saw it. 'Yes,' I said.

Her mother's first reaction was, 'Oh my god, she's not going to die is she?'

I shook my head. 'No, the doppelganger isn't hers. It's not something her own soul has created.' I tuned in again to double-check what was there.

Belinda was drifting in and out of sleep. When she next opened her eyes, I held her hand and said, 'Belinda, can you think of anyone who'd want to put a curse on you?'

It took her a few minutes to digest this information and to think about it.

'Well, yes, maybe,' she said in a faint voice, as she began to recall several details that fell into place.

Once this kind of curse-energy has been identified it can be dealt with accordingly. I cleared the doppelganger and the next day I got a call from Belinda's mum saying she was recovering beautifully.

There are significant karmic implications for people who create these kinds of curses. It may sound clichéd but the saying, 'what goes around comes around' is true. People who put curses on others will have to deal with the consequences of their actions sooner or later. That's karma for you; it is a fair system. If you do something that has a low or negative vibration, eventually your soul will have to balance it out with a lesson or opportunity to create a positive vibration.

If you feel or see your own doppelganger, don't fear it. Don't presume you're going to have bad luck, get sick or die. If you buy into the negative thoughts you can actually create the bad luck you fear, or make yourself sick. Use your sixth sense to read the energy, then see if you can clear it. If you don't feel you can do it on your own ask your guides to step in and clear it for you.

Sometimes people do see their doppelganger and they do die. If you see your own doppelganger seek advice from your Spirit guide. Ask them to confirm that what you are seeing is a real doppelganger. If it is, then this is because in this case the doppelganger is actually the death mantle which sets in three days before death. This type of doppelganger has been created by your own karma because it is your time to leave this world. Your Spirit guide will help you find a way of working through this transition stage to death by giving you comfort and support.

Phantom energies are thought-created energies. They don't come into play on their own. Someone, somewhere, has created them. These energies are drawn from the ethers. It's amazing that such things can be created, but they can. They look and feel real and their impact certainly leaves its mark. It's wise to remember that we're usually the ones who've created them so watch what you ask for! It's also reassuring to know that if you're on the receiving end of a phantom energy that it can be dissolved and you can get on with your life.

45

A Walk in the Clouds

Escaping into a fantasy world is always a welcome getaway from the pressures of daily life. That's why we daydream—to break out of the monotony of routine and tantalise our senses with the feel-good factor that comes with imagining what could be. Daydreams are inspiring waking dreams that let us explore possibilities. Anything and everything is possible because you are the creative writer and director of your fantasy. There, playing out as vivid images in your personal movie, are scenes unfolding the way you want them to. And we can all do with a good dose of that at times!

Daydreams can be very constructive because they're a form of creative visualisation. So when you're daydreaming you're taking one of the first steps towards manifesting the things you want in life.

Every time you visualise yourself doing something, you're creating an energy matrix for future events. And, as you know, whatever you think and feel creates your reality. So your daydreams aren't a waste of time; they can be the foundation for things to come—provided that you do eventually take some action.

I hear many people complain that they don't have enough time in their busy lives for daydreaming, and that's a real pity. I feel daydreams are important to our psyche. We can all use a walk in the clouds—a little 'me time'. It's during these precious moments away from day-to-day responsibilities that you can reclaim inspiration, passion, desire and hope. I know the philosophy of living in the moment is popular, and I agree that some truly wonderful benefits are derived from doing this, being aware of what you're doing while you're doing it allows you to extract the most from each and every minute. But if we don't spend some time thinking about the future, or working on clearing the past, can we really move forwards? Live in the moment, cherish its gifts, but please also allow yourself time to daydream. Investing time on harnessing your positive thoughts can work wonders.

Tracey was a single parent and struggling financially and also with trying to find her direction in life.

She told me, 'I would sit in my lounge room daydreaming of a better life. I would often daydream and see myself working for the Department of Community Services. When I started doing this I never really believed it would come true but, the more I had the daydream, the more I focused on making it a reality. I began making changes to my life. I enrolled in relevant courses and completed two diplomas. Then I completed my Bachelor of Arts. I am now where I dreamed I would be. I have a job that I love as a domestic violence specialist helping women in need.'

One morning my dog Bodo wanted me to take him for a walk. Spring was in the air with blossoms and new leaves sprouting. Off we went down the street and through the park and I had to stop near a tree full of delicious white blossoms and lose myself for a few moments in their wonderful aroma. A gentle breeze brushed against me and the sun kissed my skin. Time stopped. It was a perfect moment, rich and sublime. I felt genuinely happy. Then I looked up at the sky and noticed a few clouds floating by. They reminded me of how quickly opportunities passed. I lay down on the grass and watched the clouds morphing against the backdrop of the blue sky. I imagined myself floating up there and looking down at my body, at the park, at the suburb.

Life is transient and we waste so much time sweating the small stuff and losing precious moments. So I let myself daydream. I was living my fantasy of jumping onto the world stage and educating people about psychic and spiritual development. This has been my passion, and I have been following it through with my work and by making appearances at festivals and in the media. I'll keep daydreaming to keep things moving forwards. I find such dreams both healing and beneficial. They help me map out the steps I need to take to make my life goals come true. During these daydreaming times I also use my sixth sense to give me a glimpse of the future. Once I get my inspirational vision I can spend a few minutes living it and helping it take shape as a very real possibility.

There are other benefits to daydreaming aside from getting in touch with your soul's desire. Daydreaming gives your brain time to incorporate what you're learning about life. It can help you to absorb and understand experiences and even begin to resolve problems while your thoughts are relaxed and focused elsewhere.

Creative visualisation is a powerful tool. Unleash your fantasies and give them the opportunity to become real.

46

I'm Into You—Really!

The delicious thing about daydreaming is that you're using visualisation to create the future you want. It also improves your wellbeing. If you're feeling stressed you can visualise yourself relaxing on a tropical island and this will calm you down. Or, if you're dealing with an illness, you can visualise all the cells in your body being restored back to perfect health. You can also use visualisation to shapeshift.

Shapeshifting involves metamorphosis or transmogrification, which means to change form by 'magic'. With your sixth sense ability you can shift into something like a rock, animal, tree or Spirit to gain a deeper awareness of the world. You do this through visualisation by visualising the form you wish to merge into and then astrally projecting your awareness into it. Essentially, you are shifting from human form into another, becoming an intrinsic part of the natural world. It's an incredible experience.

You can shapeshift into anything you want while you are in the astral plane. You can explore what it feels like to be the wind, or to take on the awareness of an ancient tree, or of an animal guide to help you learn its ways. You can also use it as a vehicle to explore the Spirit world.

Native Americans shapeshifted by taking on the Spirit of their prey to ensure a successful hunt. They would also shapeshift to take on the qualities and strengths of individual animals. If you're facing challenges it may help you to draw on the unique power of an animal Spirit for a short time. If you feel the need to embody the Spirit of a warrior, you might choose to shapeshift into a creature such as a bear. Bears are considered to be unpredictable, powerful and courageous, true warrior spirits. In the Amazon warriors become jaguars to travel soundlessly through the jungle. If you want to be creative and think outside the box you might prefer to shapeshift into a light-hearted sparrow. The sparrow has a different kind of power to the bear. It gains its strength and protection from being part of a group. Being a master of flight this bird also draws in higher ideas and creativity which may help you to solve other problems.

Shapeshifting can also be used in healing. Some shamans or energy healers are known to shapeshift into their patient so they can see what's really going on inside their body. Or they may travel to the Spirit world to bring back insights such as what medicines will help heal their patient. It is said that certain medicine men 'ingest' the energy of an illness from their patient, then release the energy to cure them.

Shapeshifting can occur on three different levels:

- Cellular—this is where you transform from human to plant or animal consciousness. Plants have amazing healing qualities. Imagine being able to shapeshift into a plant to discover its therapeutic qualities for yourself. Or perhaps you've got a sick plant or dog that you want to help. Shapeshifting into them for a few minutes can give you an insight into exactly what they need to heal.

- Personal—this is where you adopt new attributes or characteristics to help you become a new person. Say you're a very fixed person and you need to become a little more mutable. Shapeshifting into the consciousness of a river can help you get a feel for how to flow with things because water naturally adapts and meanders around its environment.
- Institutional—use the power of a group to gain insight into life. Imagine shapeshifting into a collective to understand their take on things? Whether it's a collective of bees to get a sense of community, or into a collective Spirit to gain creative inspiration, you can expand your awareness and become innovative.

A shapeshifter can also be called a skin-walker or transformer. In folklore many mythical and supernatural beings are said to have shapeshifting abilities. Most cultures have some kind of transformation myth buried in their collective consciousness. Stories of gods and goddesses coming down to the earth and adopting animal form, or merging into the natural kingdom, are common themes in humankind's stories. In some myths shapeshifting goes one step further. Instead of someone projecting themselves and sharing the animal's consciousness, they actually morph into the animal itself to disguise their presence from enemies. In Celtic myth, shapeshifting is employed regularly for survival, protection, punishment or to facilitate rebirth.

If you feel like trying your hand at shapeshifting, try this exercise.

Close your eyes and take a deep breath in and slowly exhale. Take another deep breath in and exhale. Clear your mind and let your body relax. When you are ready focus on an animal you wish to shapeshift into. It is important to always get its permission first. Ask for this permission and then visualise yourself becoming this animal for a short time. Feel what it's like to be in the animal's body, take on its posture, its movements, its characteristics. Get the animal to guide you through its world and see what you discover.

How wonderful it is to be able to use your sixth sense to merge into the world around you. But a word of caution—be careful not to take on another form for too long, especially when you're just starting out. Start off with an hour or so, then later on let your sixth sense tell you how long is ideal for you. If you choose to take on the form of a lion, for example, you'll take on its positive traits; but if you remain focused on the lion-form for too long you're liable to take on its shadow qualities as well.

47

Where are Your Friends When You Need Them?

Your Spirit guides don't need to shapeshift to enter your world. Spirit guides are like guardian angels. You have two kinds of Spirit guides looking after you. 'Life' guides are Spirit guides who stand by you from birth to death. The other guides, which I call 'transient guides', are the ones who come into your life on an 'as required' basis. Some of your transient guides are family and friends in Spirit who check in on you because they love and care about you. Other transient guides are not connected to your spiritual family network and may be complete strangers who come to help you because they have special skills or knowledge gained through their past lives which can be of benefit to you.

Several years ago I had a table at a local psychic fair, where I was creating Spirit guide drawings. A middle-aged lady sat down and told me she was really keen to find out who her

Spirit guide was but she was also a little sceptical. I tuned in and started drawing her guide who looked exactly like d'Artagnan, the most famous character in *The Three Musketeers*. When I finished the drawing the Spirit told me his name was Gérard. I made the silly mistake of spelling it in the English manner on the drawing (without the accent) . . . and didn't that get him going!

'It's Gérard, my little one, it's Gérard! You must tell her that I have corrected you. I help her with her French lessons, you know. I am an expert of the beautiful language of my day,' he announced.

I thought, 'Is this guy for real?'

'Ah, of course I'm real,' he quipped, reading my mind. 'I lived in France in the 1700s, so I think I should know my French very well, thank you madame.'

My client took her picture and smiled, telling me she loved how he looked. I then pointed out that our little Spirit companion was quite adamant that I tell her that he was an expert in eighteenth-century French.

She raised her eyebrows in surprise, 'That's so amazing!' she said. 'I'm studying eighteenth-century French at university right now.'

We attract Spirit guides who have the knowledge and skills to help us in different areas of our life. If you want specialist advice, why hunt through the yellow pages when you can ask your Spirit guide day or night. And better still—they're free!

A student once asked me, 'Haven't Spirit guides got anything better to do?' It was a good question. Spirit guides don't consider their role of mentor a prison sentence. They've chosen this role as part of their own spiritual growth, and they are still growing—just like we are.

If you want to feel your connection to your guides, set some time aside at night before you go to sleep, when you've let go of the concerns of the day, and ask someone you know to visit you. Relax and stay open and see if you can feel them standing next to you. Sometimes you can feel them because they brush your hair with their hand, or even touch your face as a display of their affection.

Another brilliant way of connecting with your Spirit guides is to meditate. Most people know meditation is fantastic for stress relief and relaxation but it can do so much more for you. It works wonders in creating a sense of inner stillness, which gives you the perfect platform to open your sixth sense and connect with your guides. Once you've established this connection, feel free to ask them whatever you like. Trust me, they're listening.

The thing to remember about your Spirit guides is that out of sight does not mean out of action. You might not always see your guides, but they see you. And if they can't get their message to you during the day, they'll do their best to get your attention while you dream. Your guides are here. Let them help you on your journey.

48

Lifting the Veil

Imagine being able to work with your own Gérard? I know lots of people would like to but for them the Spirit world feels as though it's a million miles away. They feel blocked and can't seem to connect with it. But, you can learn how to lift the veil that separates you from your Spirit guides. How? By shifting your awareness away from the logical left brain way of seeing things and into the intuitive right mode. This opens you up to connecting with your guides. You see a lot of your intuitive impressions come directly to you from your Spirit guides. When you are open, it is picked up by your sixth sense and passed on. If you are closed no information gets through to your mind because you are stuck in the logical mind.

Children are particularly open channels and they pick up information all the time. Sometimes they see their guides, referring to them in such ways as 'my special friend' which parents usually refer to as 'imaginary friends'. Other times, children don't see anything, but they still get impressions, thoughts and ideas directly from their guides.

When Eva was five, she couldn't see her guides, but they were working alongside her. 'We were sitting in the living room with my family. My mum had her feet resting underneath a lamp. A thought ran through my mind, "What if the lamp falls down on Mami's feet and breaks them?" Only a few seconds later, it actually happened. My mum was in pain and her feet were bleeding.'

•

You can talk with your loved ones in Spirit when you need some advice on a personal matter. At twenty-two Eva's guides came to help warn her again. 'It came like a short movie running through my head. I saw myself having a misunderstanding with my boyfriend and after that he told me he had slept with another woman. The tears welled in my eyes. The next day my boyfriend and I saw each other and all of a sudden the movie became real—we had a misunderstanding and he admitted an indiscretion. My guides had been trying to prepare me. They cared enough to do that for me.'

Not long after, Eva's guides helped her make a major decision. 'I had just finished my studies and I wanted to live in a foreign country, so I applied for internships in places like France and England. All of sudden I got this impression that I should travel to Australia. It was my dream as a child but I had forgotten about it. The feeling was so strong and loud in my head—I had to follow it. I went to an agency that specialised in travel to Australia and that night made a decision—I was going to go! Four years down the track I still absolutely love it. I've met fantastic people and the experience (including the spiritual one) can't be compared to anything else. I feel like I belong here.'

You have so many enthusiastic helpers out there. They're waiting for your call.

•

Over the years I have encountered numerous lost souls. It kind of goes with the territory. What have I learned from these encounters? That life is a lot more mysterious than I realised. Once upon a time I thought that what other people told me was 'real' had to be the truth and all the little visions I saw were products of my overactive imagination.

'Dead people don't talk!' I was told by well-meaning family and friends. But they did talk, to me at least, and eventually I became aware I wasn't a delusional lunatic at all, that my senses were spot on. I was seeing what I now call the layering effect—a world immersed within another world. I was in the throes of an awakening to life that existed beyond the veil.

It's odd how I was having a life-changing awakening due to my sixth sense yet I couldn't bring myself to use the word 'psychic'. Instead, I notched up every event to the growing list of 'weird experiences' that peppered my life. Thankfully I eventually opened myself up to these experiences and they have since helped me live a more amazing, inspirational life than I ever could have imagined. You can have this life too, if you want it.

If you feel you have a premonition of any kind, don't immediately dismiss it. Premonitions are very real phenomena. Instead, why don't you pause for a moment and focus on what you see in your premonition and feel whether it is real or not.

Don't try to rationalise what you've seen; cold logic and the sixth sense work on different wavelengths. We all have a part of us, our higher self, that knows the answer to everything we're experiencing, so why not let that part of you do the talking instead of your logical mind?

Sometimes we don't see a premonition, we simply feel or hear it. This story from Nada explains what I mean.

'Mum has a painting of Saint Therese in her home, at the top of the stairs. She absolutely believes that Saint Therese's painting changes from time to time; that is, some days she looks happy and other days she looks sad and even has a tear in her eye. Whenever Mum notices the sadness, she asks Saint Therese to tell her why. And every time Saint Therese has spoken to Mum, the message has been accurate.

'One message Mum received was about me. She was told that I was going to get sick and that I would divorce my husband. When Mum told me this several months later, I was surprised as I had still not told her about either my illness (water on the lung) or that I was leaving my husband, as I didn't want to worry her or Dad.

'Mum's intuition is getting stronger each day and she is learning to trust what Saint Therese is telling her. I think in the beginning she was hesitant to tell me her insights in case I would think she was crazy. I told her I believed her and that all is possible, and to keep trusting what she heard, even if it was sad news.'

•

If you feel a premonition, stop for a moment and clear your mind. When you're mind is still, focus on your body and listen to what it has to say. Your body has its own 'intelligence' and senses what's real or not. Trust your 'gut feeling'. If you still feel uneasy, if you feel that something is wrong, then it probably is.

It's hard to know what is going to happen in the future especially when you get a feeling but can't see any clear images. Your intuition will give you the right information if you stay open to it. Ask questions such as, 'How is this event going to affect me?' or 'When is this event going to happen?', and even, 'What can I do about it?'

The most important thing to understand about premonitions is that you are being warned. Premonitions give you the opportunity to be prepared, and this can create a sense of empowerment, even if an event is beyond your control.

49

Because We Need Them

It's reassuring knowing that your Spirit guides are always by your side. Whether they're helping by triggering premonitions, giving answers in dreams or holding your hand on sleepless nights, they never miss a beat. We don't always give credit to these diligent and beautiful helpers, especially the angelic ones.

Angels are as much a part of our life as the air we breathe. Yet so many people are sceptical of their existence. I've also met plenty of people who believe in angels but who feel they keep their distance from mere mortals and only visit a select group of chosen ones. But what if it was the other way around? What if angels are around us all of the time, patiently listening to our hopes, wishes and prayers? Tune in and you'll discover this to be true—they're everywhere! Angels don't have a monopoly on graveyards and cathedrals, look carefully and you'll find that they are entangled in your everyday life. They watch over you while you sleep, they're with you during difficult periods at work, you'll find them in the hospital when you visit a sick friend, and don't be surprised to find them walking hand in hand with you along the beach. Perhaps you've felt their presence around you when you've needed them most? I know many people who believe they've got a guardian angel around them even though they can't see or feel them.

Let the angels know what you need and they will help you manifest it. If it's healing you are after, or if you are looking for a miracle to turn your life around, seek their assistance and you'll never regret it.

I had a friend who was drowning in a personal crisis I call 'the dark night of the soul.' Everything was crumbling around her and she was feeling lost and alone and unable to find safe ground anywhere.

'I didn't think I could tell people about my own private hell,' she told me later. 'But god, I wish someone could have hugged me or waved a magic wand to make everything ok. But nobody did. I swear I felt empty and insignificant and I thought I was going under.

'I prayed and prayed for help and just kept on praying until I felt the presence of something in my room and the word "angel" jumped into my head. I know it was there, I'm sure I didn't imagine it because I sensed a change in the atmosphere around me. In my mind I saw a vision of an angel embracing me and I felt a shift. Deep inside me I saw one word: "faith". It was illuminated like a lighthouse and I knew then that everything was going to be all right. I honestly believe that the angel's touch gave me faith and I know I haven't got the right words to describe how it felt but it was a kind of bliss that came out of thin air.'

Angels are extraordinary. They can see our thoughts and feelings and reach into our soul. These winged messengers don't just see you or me; they see everyone and know where humanity is heading. They know us and know how to apply a spiritual salve to heal our wounds.

There is no stock standard angel, it would be a mistake to lump them altogether because they are as diverse as we are. I don't mean that angels have individuality or personalities like we do—rather, they have a lot of diversity in their form and function. And, while most people see them as they are depicted in popular culture or religious artworks—serenely beautiful human-like beings with wings—please note that some angels are formless. Instead of bodies shaped like people, these angels are made up of splendid bursts of luminous colour flowing in the most amazing configurations. Speaking in the fire language, angels come in all shapes and sizes. You name it, there is an angel for every occasion who'll stand by you and give you healing, messages, protection, guidance, joy and inspiration—whatever it is you need. If you let them in they'll give you the answers you're looking for. They've got an endless supply of divine energy to change your world.

I like to think of angels as 'engineers' who come down to earth to help in human development. Whether you are an atheist or a believer, angels don't take sides or judge; they simply care enough about humanity to help us awaken to our own inner light.

50

I Could Use a Little TLC

The body's intrinsic intelligence is faultless. Picking up on subtle changes, it is able to send out warning signals before an illness or disease kicks in. Your body registers changes in your wellbeing before your conscious mind becomes alert to it. You can do yourself a lot of good by tuning in, and listening, to your body.

Most of us will listen to the fluttering butterflies in our stomach. It's a clear sign that we're feeling uneasy or disempowered. Your gut feeling—whether we feel good about something or not—is an internal barometer, a gauge telling you what is really happening inside you. People often follow their gut instincts without knowing why, but when they do the instinct is usually right.

Years ago my brother Joe went to see his doctor after experiencing rectal bleeding. The doctor told Joe there was nothing to worry about and the bleeding was simply caused by haemorrhoids. But Joe's gut instinct told him otherwise and he pressed the doctor to explore the matter further. Initially the doctor resisted his request but Joe was adamant, 'I want it investigated.'

A colonoscopy revealed polyps and a biopsy was taken. The specialist told him, 'You're so lucky you came when you did. If you had waited another month it would have turned cancerous.'

What if you could go one step further—to skip the pain and heartache of disease by being one step ahead? You can, by just listening to your body.

To diagnose a condition that hasn't fully manifested into your physical body, look for energy blocks in your aura—especially murky orange or russet-coloured blocks. Note where a block is located and in which chakra, and you'll start getting clues as to where in the physical body an illness or disease is more likely to manifest. Let's say that you discover an energy block hovering in the emotional body right over the liver area. This indicates that you're holding on to a lot of suppressed anger or frustration. Metaphysically, the liver is where we store these particular emotions.

Here is a list of the emotions commonly stored in specific organs, and their underlying causes:

- The emotions behind liver problems are anger, frustration and resentment. The underlying cause comes from a lack control or a feeling of disempowerment.
- The emotions behind stomach problems stem from uncertainty. The underlying cause comes from feeling sad, or the inability to emotionally or psychologically digest an idea or issue. A lack of confidence or joy can also create stomach problems.

- Problems in the kidneys are generally created because you are feeling guilty. It often plays out because you are finding it hard to let go of the past and family issues.
- If you have health issues around the breast area it indicates a lack of self nurture or that you are giving out too much love and not receiving enough in return.
- When you get tension headaches around the brow, or your eye sight gets blurry, ask yourself, 'what is it that I cannot let myself see?'

A complete list of how stored emotions affect your different organs and wellbeing is available on my website <http://suebishoponline.com>.

The liver organ comes under the solar plexus chakra, which is our empowerment centre. So, if we put this together with our knowledge of which emotions are associated with the liver, our sixth sense is telling us that, 'You're really angry because you don't feel that you have any control over an area of your life.' Tune in and your sixth sense will help you identify which area of your life is problematic. The point is that you're holding on to anger that's not being given an opportunity to be expressed properly. Sometimes we repress emotions because we tell ourselves we're ok with a situation when we're really not. If we were we wouldn't have an energy block.

If you explore any underlying emotional, psychological and spiritual issues that you're holding on to, you can potentially stop an illness in its tracks before it takes hold of your body. Once you've identified the affected area, try to understand the issue for what it is. This is such an important step in the healing process. By having an understanding of why things are, it's so much easier to dissolve and let go of energy blocks.

Recognising and working to resolve emotional issues will help you keep your energy field healthy.

But what if you misread your body's intuitive signals, or your body fails to warn you? Some illnesses and diseases are meant to be because they're karmic. Your sixth sense or, for that matter, your guides, might not tell you because it's in keeping with your karma to experience a particular illness or disease at a particular time. Karmic conditions can override our free will. Use the experience to learn about yourself.

A karmic illness or disease is triggered by miasms. In his book *Vibrational Medicine*, Dr Richard Gerber says, 'Miasms are energetic tendencies which predispose an individual toward manifesting particular illnesses.' In other words there's a karmic (genetic) potential to experiencing a disease. At a certain point in your life your soul activates the miasm which triggers the body's chemistry, to send out instructions on what disease needs to manifest, where it manifests and what level of severity it will reach. This is all in keeping with our soul's bigger plan so don't look at it as bad luck or misfortune.

What about chronic conditions? What can you do to heal yourself if you were born to experience a particular condition?

I see illness and disease as learning platforms for our growth. I tell people the intensity of an illness reflects the degree of separation from self-love we're experiencing at a deep emotional, psychological and spiritual level. It can be a reward in disguise because it's offering you a lesson in self-care. Healing is an expression of self-love because when you fall sick you're forced to take care of yourself. Sure, you may require medical intervention, but if you add a little self-TLC it can make a world of difference to how you recuperate.

Giving yourself TLC can include having some down time from work, spending time doing the small things in life that give meaning to you, or letting others nurture you. I find the best kind of TLC looks after the body, mind and soul. Having emotional, psychological and spiritual healing works wonders because all aspects of you are being looked after, not just your body.

You can use your sixth sense to get in touch with a different kind of healer while still utilising modern medicine. It's called angelic healing and it's a beautiful healing technique that's guaranteed to give you all the TLC you need. Here's what you do:

Close your eyes. Take a deep breath, and slowly breathe out. Take another deep breath and slowly exhale, feeling your body relax more with every deep breath you take. When you are ready, ask for a healing angel to come to your assistance. Use your sixth sense to visualise a luminous angel standing in front of you. Feel its presence and open your heart. Give your body permission to accept healing without reservation.

Ask the angel to send down a ray of divine, healing blue light all over you and feel this energy dissolving any restrictive thoughts and feelings that you've been hanging on to. Peel back any illness and disease and you will find an underlying thought or feeling beneath it. Clear away thoughts or patterns that no longer serve you.

When you are ready, draw this healing ray into every cell in your body. Ask this energy to flush out all emotional and psychological toxins. Then direct the blue light into the affected area of your body and feel the angelic energy giving you healing. Allow this to sweep through you then visualise the angel sending you healing pink energy. Absorb it until your intuition tells you that you've received enough. Finish off with a lovely, vibrant green energy. Absorb it into every cell in your body until you feel your body getting stronger and healthier.

Thank the healing angel for their time.

Always get a medical diagnosis and treatment options for any worrying symptoms. And don't be afraid to insist if you feel any further investigation is required.

51

Ouch! That Hurt!

Voodoo might be an alluring name for a perfume, but the practice of voodoo doesn't come up smelling like roses—it's a form of psychic attack. Psychic attacks are energy-based assaults on your soul and can include spells, curses and hexes. In some cultures it's not uncommon to hear of someone placing the evil eye on a person to trigger misfortune. Psychic attacks are disruptive; there's no doubt about that when you meet someone who has been on the receiving end. An attack can last a day, week, a year or even a lifetime if it's not removed. Some curses can carry on through generations until someone in the family breaks the link. Although most people don't talk about this sort of thing, and it's not common, it does happen. Why suffer at the hands of someone else's negativity? Having an understanding of how curses and other forms of psychic attack work will empower you and help you to clear these energies.

As much as I'd love to wear rose-coloured glasses and tell myself people aren't cruel and malicious, the truth is some people are. They want to disrupt people's lives because of their own pain and discontent, and may even visit dubious 'consultants' who can cast hexes and spells for them.

Some people don't realise casting spells is invasive. But the truth is, even if you're using white magic or trying to do a positive thing, interfering with someone's free will is not right.

For those with less-innocent intentions, an evil eye, curse or hex is cast through some form of ritual or projection of an intention. Working with focused thoughts and invoking the elements of earth, water, fire and air, these psychic attackers send out a negative projection or attachment to the person they want to harm.

I know how powerful psychic attacks can be. A few years ago I experienced one first-hand and was surprised to find out how cunning and sinister some people can be. The person attacking me wanted to disrupt my life because of professional jealousy. I had my usual level of psychic protection up, and for the most part my protection was working and my aura was clear. But my adversary cleverly created a phantom energy effigy of me looking pale, sickly and with a noose around my head, and I kept seeing it when I tuned in. They were trying to make me think suicidal thoughts. And strangely enough I was beginning to feel severely depressed. When I discovered this attack, I asked my guides, 'How did this get to hang around me? Why didn't you warn me?' They told me that I had needed to understand more about the dynamics of psychic attack. I had mistakenly thought I was okay because I couldn't find any hooks in my aura, but the reality was that having been unable to get into my aura, my adversary had gone a step further and created the effigy to cut me down.

The effects of a curse, spell or hex can be devastating. In the past I've been called to help people who've suffered great misfortune and ill health because they've been the victims of psychic attacks. The good news is that psychic attacks can be broken. You can defend yourself, your home, your family and friends. You can also create a protective barrier to stop further attacks from harming you. (And it's worth mentioning that this darkness always rebounds on the attacker due to karma because they are causing harm to others.)

You must also be careful that you don't unwittingly cause your own psychic attack. If you repeatedly focus on the same negative thoughts about a person then you'll create a mild form of psychic attack. So be careful. I've recently found a workable solution to unintentionally causing this type of attack. I white-light my thoughts with the intent that, should I think or feel negatively towards other people, this white-light energy dissolves the negative thought before it can cause any disruption. This way, I get to honour how I feel but I don't cause any harm to others. You can do this for yourself.

No one should have to suffer because of the negative acts of other people. But unless you know what to look for, and understand how psychic attacks work, you're stumbling in the dark. Let your sixth sense tell you when adverse energies are being directed at you so you can do something to protect yourself. If you think you are on the receiving end of a spell, hex, curse or evil eye, seek professional advice on how to clear the problem yourself, or ask a professional to do it for you.

Don't let psychic attacks get the better of you. Put your mind at ease by putting up a bit of psychic protection.

What you can do

A simple yet effective technique to protect yourself that works wonders is to start your day by stating your intention that you wish to be protected.

- At the start of each day, before you step out of your front door, simply visualise a column of white light washing down over your entire aura.
- Ask for a net of protective golden energy to wash down over your aura, energetically sealing and protecting you.
- Ask that this light maintain the integrity of your aura, so you can stay open to your intuition, and to feeling and getting messages, but without absorbing other people's energies, or attracting unwanted beings.
- If you feel you're under attack from negative thoughts, use this technique first, then visualise mirrors facing outwards from your aura. Ask that these mirrors reflect any negative thoughts or energy back to its place of origin.

52

When My Guides Stepped In

It is reassuring to know that you can be protected from unwanted energies. Spirit can protect you in the most extraordinary ways. Have you ever felt them watching over you? Maybe your partner or a friend has talked about such an experience? People find comfort from knowing their Spirit guides are always watching over them and taking action when they need it most.

My Spirit guides have come to my rescue so many times. I'd like to tell you how they alerted me to danger on one occasion when I was twenty-eight.

I stepped off the train on the dodgy side of an inner-city suburb. I'd never alighted at this station before and by the time I'd walked through the exit darkness was setting in. Minutes later I was waiting for my boyfriend and his friend at the side of a major road. I was only about two hundred metres from the station when I was approached by two teenage girls. They asked if I had five dollars. I didn't. They walked away, but a few minutes later a voice in my head started telling me to move. 'Move now!' it urged several times. I was standing on a busy road, but in a poorly lit area and when the voice next urged me 'Move towards the station!' I listened. I was within a hundred metres of the station entrance when I was grabbed from behind and felt a blow to the side of my face. The two teenage girls were back. One tugged at my handbag, the other roughed me up. It's not in my nature to get physically aggressive, so I tried to break free. A hand ripped out one of my earrings, then tore my top. I finally escaped and they chased me to the station entrance where I called out for help. They caught up to me and threw a few punches before two men came to my rescue.

In telling me to move, my guides were giving me one form of psychic protection—they were trying to get me out of physical harm's way. Guides try their best to get messages through to you so you can avoid danger. But if you're not listening, they can't barge in and override your free will. And unless you ask for protection, they can't give it. If you want them to step in and help break psychic attacks, or remove attachments like lost souls or phantom energies, ask your guides for help.

Beginners don't have to get into complicated rituals or mantras. As you develop your sixth sense your guides will enjoy more interaction with you. They'll encourage you to take gradual steps towards standing on your own two feet and work with you in protecting yourself. And energetic protection is where they really shine!

I feel it's important to add that sometimes your guides will let something slip through the protective net. Anything that gets through is meant to help you grow in awareness. One of my most talented students, Jenny, overcame a lot of fears because the odd challenging being would break through her protection.

When she asked her guides why this happened, they told her it was because it helped her to understand what different energies felt like. She learned so much from confronting such beings and now uses that knowledge and wisdom to help her own clients and students. Challenges are usually blessings in disguise. It doesn't matter what situation you find yourself in. Help is always on hand. The wonderful thing about working with your guides is that they are an endless source of love, help and protection.

53

Protect Yourself

It never ceases to amaze me how strong and powerful energetic protection is once it has been put in place. One of the fundamental principles of working with energy or psychic awareness is to protect your energies from any negative or invasive influences. But you have to remember to do it! You can ask the guardians of light to protect and seal your home so you can do your psychic work in the safety and comfort of their protection, and you can learn to recognise dangers such as energy vampirism.

Years ago, my sister Frances and I were visiting a sick relative in hospital. Frances suddenly said, 'I don't feel right.'

'What's wrong?' I asked.

'I feel tired. I'm dizzy and tired.' I grabbed a chair for her. 'This is crazy,' she said as she flopped into the chair and asked for water. 'I was feeling happy before I got in here but now I can hardly move. I'm feeling totally drained and nauseous!' The colour had drained from her cheeks. 'I want to go home and get some sleep. It's weird. Why do hospitals always do this to me?'

What Frances didn't realise was that she had fallen victim to what is commonly called an 'energy vampire'. Energy vampires are people who drain your energy. Most energy vampires don't realise they're doing it and have no negative intentions towards you. For many it's merely a temporary phase when their own energy is so low that they unconsciously take some of yours to top themselves up. Perhaps you've experienced this first-hand while visiting a sick friend? Maybe it's happened when you were standing next to your tired mum, or when you're standing next to a really stressed out co-worker? One moment you're feeling fantastic then suddenly, wham, the life is knocked out of you.

'Frances,' I said. 'You're too open.'

'What do you mean I'm too open? Open to what?'

'Energy . . . other's people's stuff. You've allowed yourself to be drained.'

She lifted an eyebrow in surprise. 'What are you talking about? Why would I do that?'

'Because you don't know how to protect yourself from what others are feeling. You're sensitive to energy. I know you don't like to think that you're psychic but look at you, you're always picking up on other people's feelings.'

'Yes, I know I pick up emotions, but this is different.'

'Not really. You pick up their emotions and take them on board. You're like a giant sponge soaking up other people's stuff.'

'You can say that again,' she smiled weakly.

'And you hold on to it. The only difference is that you're not taking their energy because you're low on it yourself. You merge your energies with them and feel what they feel. They don't feel what you feel they simply take your energy to give themselves a top up.

'That's what happens when you're energetically open. The upside is that you can really empathise and feel compassion for others, but the downside is that sometimes they'll drain you when they're feeling low on energy themselves.'

She looked over at our relative in bed. 'Oh, I get it now. He's wiped out, and so he's taking my energy.'

I nodded. 'Yes, he's being a bit of a vampire at the moment. But it's only because he doesn't know how to get a top up of energy for himself, and that's why he's taking yours.'

'Well, why isn't he making everyone else here tired?'

'Because the others aren't as open as you are, and I've already protected myself. I'll show you. Close your eyes and relax for a moment.'

I channelled an uplifting healing energy into her for a few minutes. 'How do you feel now?'

'A lot better.'

Frances now recognises the signs of energy vampirism and immediately tops up her own energies and also puts up her own protection.

If you're feeling low on energy, or if you're feeling drained because of someone else, you need to top up your own energy reserves. To do this you draw energy down from the universe through your transpersonal point and up from the earth through your earth star chakra until you feel revitalised. Visualise a luminous bluish-white light filled with revitalising energy washing down over you. Feel it moving into every cell of your body until you feel topped up. Then perform the same white light and golden grid protection exercise I've included on page 196.

A word of warning: there are a few energy vampires who do know what they're doing, and for them it's a power trip. If you feel you've been zapped by one, top up your own energies first, then use the reflective mirror protection technique.

54

Energy Stuff

The exquisite part of working with energy is its simplicity. Universal and earth energy are pure sources of power, there's nothing complicated about them. The only thing that complicates energy is how our own thoughts and feelings interact with it. Energy just follows our lead. We command it and it does what it's told to do. How and when it plays out depends on your personal karma. If you stick with the basics you'll find working with energy easy. All you have to remember is to keep your thoughts and intentions simple and clear. The energy you create will reflect this.

There's an endless supply of universal energy so there is always enough to go around. This energy will take on any quality you want. Say you can't shake a cold, all you have to do is say, 'Please send me some healing energy,' and visualise a lovely blue light washing down over you. That's all it takes.

I remember being really sick one day when the kids were little. I couldn't get out of bed, I was dizzy, my head hurt and my chest was burning like mad. No one was on hand to help, so I decided to open up my energy to receiving healing. I lay in bed and closed my eyes and tried to take my mind off the pain. It was hard at first but I kept reminding myself that the kids needed me. I visualised the blue healing light washing over me. Every so often my mind would cut in and distract me, but I kept returning to visualising the healing energies moving through me. I don't know how long I did it for but at some point I fell asleep. When I woke up I felt so much better. The aches were down, and my chest didn't hurt as much and the headache was gone. My energy was back, I could sit up without getting dizzy. It was enough for me to get out of bed and look after the kids.

There's no need for complicated rituals. If you want to feel more empowered why not ask for some help? Ask Spirit to, 'Please send me an energy to build my confidence and personal power' and visualise a bright yellow light washing down over you.

Energy can also be used to heighten your sixth sense. I teach my students to 'open up' their energy before doing intuitive work because it increases their psychic sensitivity.

Here's a simple exercise you can do to open up.

Visualise a column of vibrant white light washing down through your transpersonal point.

Take the white light down past the base chakra and then down into the earth star. Ask that it synchronises you and expands your intuition. Draw the energy from the earth up into your earth star and ask that it brings grounding and healing energies into you. Draw the light up into your heart, feel it opening and expanding your heart chakra. Then visualise white light coming down through the crown. Take this light all the way down into your solar plexus chakra and ask that it empower you and connect you to the universe, to higher awareness and higher intuition. Visualise the light from your solar plexus moving up to connect with the heart chakra. As they connect, feel the strengthening of your alignment to the earth, to the universe, and to your higher self.

The following exercise will help you to 'close down', to protect your energy after you've finished working with your sixth sense. This procedure protects you and maintains the integrity of your energy.

Visualise a column of violet-white light over you, and then bring down a rose-gold net energy over you, asking that it seal and protect you. This helps shield you from unwanted external energies such as people's excess emotions and negative thoughts. It also protects you from attracting attachments such as lost souls into your personal space.

Learning to work with energy to manage your own energy makes sense. Whether it's to protect your energy, change moods and even heal yourself, energy is the source of power that you can use to make things happen.

55

I'm Bulletproof

Most people wouldn't dream of running out into a thunderstorm without some sort of protection like an umbrella or raincoat. Yet they leave home without giving any thought to their psychic protection. Why leave things to chance when it's so easy to protect yourself? All you need to do is to strengthen your energy field. Creating psychic protection isn't a complicated process and once you have learned how to do it you'll wonder why you didn't do it sooner.

Psychic protection helps you create a healthy boundary around your own energy, to define your personal space. This is particularly important for hypersensitive or intuitive people who are like psychic sponges that pick up everyone's energy. Placing this kind of boundary around you ensures you stay open and intuitively aware but without the downside of being reactive to your environment. It creates a perfect win-win solution.

The other thing psychic protection does is stop unwanted attachments such as negative thoughts, hooks and projections from invading your personal space. It also stops lost souls from attaching to your energy.

If a lost-soul attachment is left unattended it can, over several years, turn into a case of split personality or possession. I want to stress that this is not very common but it is something to be aware of, and a great incentive to protect your energy. I've dealt with people with lost-soul attachments and they're not difficult to remove if you remove them early on before they attach to the chakras and become embedded in your aura. If left for extended periods of time, and depending upon the personality of the lost soul, it can take a bit of effort to remove the attachment because they can resist being evicted.

I had a client called Lisa who came to see me because a telephone psychic told her she had a lost-soul attachment. Lisa couldn't feel an attachment and she didn't hear voices in her head or suffer any of the trauma that you expect from someone with an attached lost soul, but her intuition had told her she should see me.

When I tuned into Lisa's aura I saw the Spirit of a little girl enmeshed with her. I was shown she'd been with Lisa since she was ten years old—no wonder she couldn't tell there was another life force living inside her, she didn't know what it felt like not to have one! My guides told me that when she was ten Lisa's father was in hospital after suffering a heart attack.

'Yes, Dad was in hospital. He was in England on business when he suffered a heart attack and we flew over to be with him.'

While she was walking the corridor of the hospital, the lost soul of a little girl who'd died weeks earlier decided to follow Lisa home. Over time the lost soul merged her energy with Lisa's and they became one. Since it happened while Lisa was young, she never differentiated the other personality. They grew up together, although the lost soul's personality remained childlike. Lisa had always taken it to be an aspect of her own inner child.

I removed the lost soul and sent her home to be reunited with her family. Then I taught Lisa how to protect her energies to ensure she never had another attachment. I asked her to call me a week later with an update on how she was.

Lisa cried over the phone when she told me how empty she was feeling, as though part of her was missing. Well, part of her was missing—a part of her that should not have been a part of her essence to begin with. She was, however, a soul who shared Lisa's life for over twenty years. It would take Lisa some time to learn to be her own person again.

Psychic protection strengthens your energy field. It gives you a say in what is allowed in, and what is to stay out. It's reassuring to know you have the power to shield yourself from any unwanted energy. There are a number of different techniques you can use to protect yourself. Here are a few suggestions:

Mantras and prayers

A mantra is a powerful sacred invocation. It can be a single word, or a sound or phrase that creates mind protection. Mantras are widely used in Hindu and Buddhist traditions as these energy-based sounds carry a vibration to focus an intention. Their true power lies in the meaning you associate or put behind your words. For example, if you create a mantra like 'Spirit protects me,' and repeat it over and over, it creates a wave-like energy that builds this reality for you. It's a very potent form of mind protection because you believe in it and because you have invoked divine energy to protect you.

Mantras can be used to protect your health, relationships, finances, career or anything you want to protect. Prayers are very similar to mantras. People pray to God, saints or to Spirit. Prayers can be used for guidance, assistance and healing—they can be very powerful.

Talismans

A talisman or amulet is an object that has been infused with the intention to protect people from harm. Talismans can include medallions of saints, jewellery, statues and visual images. In some cultures talismans are believed to hold blessings and protective powers. You can wear a talisman on a necklace or hang it at home. In some indigenous cultures blessing are spoken over medicinal herbs to turn them into a talisman that can be consumed. The power of a talisman rests in the intentions placed into it by the person who has created it. If you're not comfortable in creating a protective talisman for yourself, you can have one specially made for you.

Energetic protection

This can be created by visualisation.

Simply clear your energy with white light. If you feel you've got something attached, like negative thought forms or hooks, then visualise a sword of fire dissolving these energies. Once your energy is clear, visualise a brilliant white light washing over you. Invoke protection (you can state your intention or use a mantra or prayer) and bring a net of golden light down over your entire aura. Then visualise a row of deflective mirrors, facing outwards, surrounding you (about a metre out) and ask that this energy repel any psychic attack.

You can ask that the negative energy returns to the place of its origin, or ask that it is neutralised before it affects anyone else. It's a kind of psychic self-defence that doesn't create any more harm, not even to the perpetrator. If you think you know who's trying to psychically attack you then you can visualise a cloak of invisibility coming over your aura that makes your energy signature invisible to that person.

Angelic protection

Feel like calling in the cavalry? Why not call on the forces of Archangel Michael to protect you from psychic attack? An angel from the lineage of Archangel Michael will protect you for as long as needed. Just remember to thank them in advance for their assistance.

Major psychic attacks are not commonplace. Mild attacks occur more often but they usually don't have a long-term impact on you. This is because they are often not a deliberately focused attack but caused by negative thoughts. Now that you know how to protect yourself, I'm sure you'll be bulletproof.

56

Don't Forget to Spring Clean

Now that you've learned to shield your personal energy, it's time to look at doing a quick spring clean of your living areas. I explained earlier how our thoughts and feelings create energies that linger within and around us. That's fine when we're feeling very positive about ourselves, with emotions such as love and joy coursing through our body. Leaving trails of that kind of energy around makes the atmosphere of a place feel good. But it's not so much of a good thing when we leave trails of energy behind when feeling negative.

It's a fact that our energy leaves an imprint on the objects we touch. If you're sitting on a lounge for a short while a thin film of your residual energy remains for a time. Residual energy contains information about us—our thoughts, feelings and our general energetic signature. People react to this subtle energy, consciously or not.

Why not try this next time you're feeling down: walk into a room full of happy people. Allow yourself to absorb their vibe and I can guarantee that you'll be uplifted pretty quickly.

Kylie called me to her apartment because she felt the presence of a ghost. Strange things had been happening like objects moving around and a presence standing by her side while she was cooking dinner. It became too noticeable to wave away. Even her sceptical partner, Dave, couldn't ignore it.

I brought a few students with me. They investigated the main living areas but were drawn to the master bedroom. After using their hands to feel the energy in the room, and their clairvoyance to get visions, I asked them what they felt was going on in the house.

'There's a lot of emotional energy,' said Maddison. 'I'm feeling anxiety in here.'

'Did anyone get anything else?' I asked.

'I'm not sure,' said Ava. 'But is there an older woman's Spirit here?'

I nodded my head. 'Ask her who she is.'

A few minutes later, Maria said, 'Kylie's grandmother.'

Ava and Maddison agreed.

I asked them for some personality traits and pieces of the grandmother's personal history to tell Kylie, to validate who we had in the bedroom. Kylie confirmed the information.

'Did she have a brother in the navy? I'm seeing a dark haired man in a navy uniform,' one of the girls said.

'Yes, she did. He served in World War Two.' Kylie turned and looked at me, 'But why is she anxious and fearful?' she asked. 'It doesn't make sense, she had a good life.'

'The girls have been picking up on your own residual energy,' I told her. 'You've been lying here at night getting anxious, haven't you?'

'Yes, yes I have, you're right,' she said looking surprised. Work issues had been making her very emotional.

I explained to the students that they were picking up two things: Kylie's grandmother's Spirit and Kylie's emotions. Kylie was releasing her emotional energy in the bedroom and her residual energy was defining the atmosphere in the apartment. You can walk into two beautiful houses but while the energy in one can make you feel right at home, the energy of the other makes you uncomfortable. Your sixth sense picks up these nuances all the time.

Have you thought about the energy you're leaving lying around the house? We know how messy a place can get when we're busy—dust builds, dirty dishes pile up—sooner or later we have to clean it or face a domestic nightmare. The same can be said about the stockpile of negative thoughts and feelings that can build up over time. The feeling of the house becomes sluggish. Is that the atmosphere you want family and friends to feel when they pop in for a visit?

Alternatively, you might have fantastic energies yourself but frequent visits from a troubled friend may begin to affect the vibe of your home. While they're telling you about their problems it's likely that they are unconsciously off-loading some of their energy into the room.

I asked my students to do a spring clean of the residual energies in Kylie's bedroom. There was no need to clear the grandmother—she wasn't a lost soul, just a caring relative in Spirit popping in to keep an eye on her stressed granddaughter.

Why not turn your hand at working with your sixth sense to change the ambience of your environment? Fill it with uplifting energy to create an atmosphere of love and tranquillity so it feels like a real home. It's easy enough to do with a little bit of energetic spring cleaning.

To remove excess and residual energies that accumulate in your home begin by visualising a column of white light in the middle of the room. If you're comfortable working with your chakras simply direct the white light from the universe down through your crown and project it out of the solar plexus chakra to create the column.

Then state your intention to remove any lingering thoughts and feelings. Visualise the column of white light turning into a vortex (like a mini tornado) in the centre of the room. Visualise it spinning slowly in a clockwise direction, picking up any negative energy as it moves.

Allow this column of energy to slowly expand until it fills the entire room, including the corners, ceiling and floor.

Ask that all negative energy be taken up into this column, and returned to the universe. Ask that it be converted into positive energy (yes, we're recycling!) that can filter back into your room.

Now let's add a bit of atmosphere. Think about the mood you want to set. You create it by drawing energy from the universe and programming it. For example, if you want to create a sense of calm, visualise the energy creating lovely spheres of blue light in the room. If you're comfortable working with the chakras then draw the universal energy into your crown chakra and then into the solar plexus. Visualise the universal energy as blue light forming a ball, and program it by asking it to create a sense of calm.

You have the power to change the energy in your environment. All it takes is a few positive thoughts and a little light. Here are the attributes of some common colours you can call on in your visualisations:

- *Red* is excellent for creating physical vitality and action, a sense of being grounded, secure and abundant. It also improves your sense of individuality. You can even use red in a healing capacity. It's great for working on blood disorders, the bones and skin.
- *Orange* is a fantastic colour for creating a great social atmosphere. It helps soothe emotions, relationship problems and inspires creativity. You can use orange to help improve food absorption through the intestines and circulation problems, and to work on lung and kidney disorders.
- If you want to make the room livelier or happier a good dose of *yellow* light works magic. It also inspires new ideas. Yellow infuses us with joy and happiness so it's no surprise that people suffering from depression are placed in yellow-coloured rooms. Yellow can also be used to heal stomach, pancreas and liver disorders.
- *Green* helps create inner harmony, self nurture and growth. This colour creates a sense of love. (If you want to up the vibe, try *pink*, it really promotes unconditional love in your environment.) As a healing ray, green works on restoring inner balance, and can be used for heart disease and hypertension.
- If you want to be more expressive, or create an environment that encourages open communication and healing then go for *blue*. It's wonderful for your creativity too. Blue helps heal thyroid and laryngeal problems.

- *Indigo* is the perfect colour to unlock your sixth sense. This colour helps your perception and vision. Use indigo to treat eye disorders.
- *Violet* inspires your higher self. It helps you to connect to all things and inspires higher awareness and understanding. Violet is a brilliant colour to use to help treat nervous and mental problems.

57

Heavenly Hot Property

We don't think twice about physically protecting our home. Whether it's an alarm, security doors, a high fence or cameras, we see the value in this kind of protection. It's comforting to know our families are safe and secure, but how often do we think about energetically protecting our home?

It's one thing to clear and protect your own energy but that alone doesn't protect your family or your home. Consider protecting your home so that everyone living in it can enjoy the benefits.

When Kaylene's three-year-old daughter Taylah started sleeping in the doorway of her room, Kaylene knew it was time to call in help. Despite being tucked into bed every night, by morning Taylah would be found in a foetal position under the doorway. When asked why she wasn't sleeping in her bed, she replied, 'Mummy. Man in my room.'

When I arrived I got Taylah to sit with her grandmother in the kitchen. I asked her to describe the man to her grandmother after I left the room and her grandmother would draw him. I walked into the bedroom with Kaylene and tuned in to see if there was a lost soul, Spirit guide or some other paranormal force in the bedroom that was making Taylah uncomfortable. Within minutes I discovered the lost soul of a dark-haired, slightly overweight man hiding in the wardrobe. He was unsettled and looked at me for answers. All he remembered was driving home late one afternoon with his two little boys sitting in the back of the car, and that was it. He was lost and couldn't find his boys anywhere, so eventually he followed Taylah and her mother home from the shops. He was also full of guilt and anxiety because he couldn't find his sons.

Lost souls do this sometimes—they attach themselves to people who seem friendly, and follow them home because they don't know where else to go. Remember, these beings are all alone. Everyone's ignoring them so they get a little desperate and try to find a safe haven in a household. You can't blame them. They're just trying to make the best out of their confusing predicament.

As it turned out this man wasn't stalking or trying to harm Taylah. He wanted to give her the fathering he was meant to be giving his boys, so he'd adopted her as his surrogate daughter. I told the lost soul that I would organise to have a doorway to the Spirit world opened for him and that his Spirit guides would appear with his little boys to welcome him. At first he didn't believe me but when the energetic doorway opened his eyes lit up—his sons were there, just as I promised.

Kaylene and I returned to the kitchen. Taylah's grandmother had finished the drawing and it was a perfect representation of the lost soul in Taylah's room. Kaylene and I did an energy clearance on the room and then on the entire house, setting up a protective sheaf over it to stop other souls from wandering in.

I gave Kaylene a follow-up call a week later and was happy to hear that since we did the clearance and protected the house, little Taylah remained safely tucked into her bed every night.

Here's how you can protect your home:

Visualise a column of luminous white light coming down from the source (you can call it the divine, the cosmos, God, whatever you relate to) and visualise it forming a vortex of energy in the middle of your home. Repeat the room-cleansing exercise from the previous chapter only instead of focusing on one room, visualise the vortex picking up unwanted residue from every room in the house. Ask that it be converted into positive energy.

You may want to call on an angel to come to your assistance for an extra boost. (If you don't want to DIY with angels, you can invoke whomever you wish to call in to do it all.)

Ask for help in creating a luminous golden light. Visualise this light encasing your entire home from the roof to under the floor. Ask the angel to energetically seal and protect your home with this golden light. Then call an angel to stand guard at the front and back entrances to your home. Ask them to stand guard over you and your family and deflect any negative energy. You can even ask that should any lost soul find its way to your house they help this being to find its way to the Spirit world. Thank the angel in advance for their work and ask them to stay as long as required with the proviso that they be freed up to do other work when they've finished helping you.

58

Thinking You Can't, but You Can

Kaylene was amazed how quickly the lost soul problem was solved. The reason everything worked out beautifully was simply this: I believe in my ability and I believe and trust in my Spirit helpers. There was nothing to block my work—no fear, uncertainty or doubt. Life's too short to waste time lingering in self-doubt. But we do. While some of us are capable of pulling ourselves out of self-doubt quickly, others find it a crippling experience. Who can blame them? Self-doubt undermines our confidence, it dents our dreams by putting them on hold on top of the 'impossible to achieve' mountain. And they'll remain there until we change our way of thinking from, 'I can't' to 'I can!' The key is you have to believe it.

Self-doubt says, 'I don't believe in me, I don't trust myself.' That's ok because we need to experience self-doubt at some stage in life to see the beauty of fragility. I call it beauty because the fragile parts of ourselves help us get in touch with our true strength. You're only as strong as your weakest point. We all have a weak point, a part of our body or personality that's imperfect. Instead of embracing these imperfections, we bury them. We think that if we hide them away deep inside no one will see our faults and we won't have to deal with this uncomfortable part of us. The soul wants us to recognise fear and uncertainty and appreciate the lesson in strength it is trying to teach us.

Shy people are genuinely surprised when I tell them, 'You were born to take centre stage.' They look at me with doubtful eyes. I explain: 'Shy people aren't born to remain shy, they're here to learn to be extroverted—to come out and shine and let people hear what they have to say.' Being heard is the one thing they fear the most; the very idea that someone might laugh at them or reject them holds them in check. You always start your journey in a place that's the opposite to where you need to end. Consequently, shy people are born to overcome self-doubt about expressing themselves, kids who are bullied at school are born to learn about leadership; experiencing self-doubt helps us to get in touch with these hidden strengths.

They say that ignorance is the playground of fear. Fear lurks behind every crevice of self-doubt. Use your sixth sense to become aware of the parts of yourself you don't know that well. Take an honest look inside.

Back in 1993 my teacher asked me if I would like to become a metaphysics teacher for her college. I seriously doubted I was teacher material. I believed students wouldn't relate to me because I was considered aloof and I felt they would judge me. I believed I couldn't do it. My soul had other ideas.

At the time we were a few days out from a famous horse race and Stephen and I were broke after purchasing our first home.

Since I doubted my teaching ability Stephen suggested I get Upstairs to confirm if I should become a teacher by giving me the winning trifecta numbers. It was a simple plan—psychically tune in and get the numbers (not realising that you weren't supposed to use your ability to win money!). My request was: 'I want proof. If I'm meant to be a teacher then let me win $15,000.' That's how much money we needed to get on top of things and get through Christmas. If we won I'd know I should accept the teaching offer and I would also learn that I should trust in my abilities.

I sat down and channelled the numbers ten, six and five. Stephen came in and said, 'Great, let me go and put money on them.' I wasn't so sure. He said, 'Look, if the numbers feel right let me go and put money on them.' Stephen felt fine about it but my lingering doubts held me back. What if my numbers were wrong?

We had planned to use my numbers and combine them with numbers my teacher was going to channel, and split the winnings. The night before the race we went to place a bet and spent $70 playing a combination of numbers. After buying the tickets we decided we'd spent too much money and downgraded our investment by half. On the day of the race I happened to be walking past the TAB when a voice inside my head urged me to play my numbers again. I dismissed the suggestion because self-doubt told me that my sixth sense wasn't crash hot. Plus, I was under the impression my teacher was playing her share of our combined numbers so it would be okay. It's amazing how the rational mind justifies things to override the sixth sense.

My numbers came up and the trifecta paid $60,000. I should have been ecstatic. But I wasn't. You see, had I trusted my abilities, and listened to Stephen's intuition we would have won $300,000.

But due to a comedy of errors—my teacher forgot to play my numbers and we'd downgraded our tickets from our original bets, we ended up winning $60,000. But, then the awful realisation hit. We'd also changed our tickets for half-price tickets! We'd successfully wiped off another $30,000. And we still had to split first prize with my teacher, even though she didn't play my numbers. In the end we made $15,000, exactly what I had asked for—$15,000 to the cent. So, after beating myself up for not trusting in my sixth sense I realised that doubting my ability came at a huge price.

What did I learn from this experience? By doubting myself I created boundaries. By not trusting in my ability I limited myself. By blocking my sixth sense I lost the opportunity to win lots of money. By not listening to my intuition I was saying, 'I don't trust in me.'

I became a teacher after that.

Are you thinking 'I can't', when you should be thinking 'I can'? Having limiting emotional and psychological beliefs is part of being human. These are perfectly naturally feelings which we all experience, but try to think of them as your learning platform. Know that you can replace them with 'I can' beliefs. 'I can' means you will reach your dreams.

•

You can use this tactic to support your sense of self.

> Start by asking questions like, 'Why do I doubt myself?' Close your eyes and ask this question. Allow images to surface in your mind. Look at the major theme that's playing out. Who,

or what situation, created the belief that, 'I'm not good enough to work with my sixth sense,' or, 'Working with the sixth sense is difficult,'? I find that most self-doubt we have stems from one or two primary sources from childhood, and in some cases from a past-life memory. Explore these avenues and let your body respond. It will let you know when you're getting close to the source because you'll feel unsettled or agitated. Distracting thoughts will try to stray you away from your focus. Look at any self-arguments that surface like, 'I'm just fooling myself.' Validate any criticism by recognising it and accepting it for what it is. Now, let it go.

Once you have found the source, replace the self-doubt with a positive belief to dissolve the restrictive one. You can try something like, 'I am a very talented person. I implicitly trust my sixth sense.' Again, allow underlying criticism to surface and acknowledge it before letting it go.

Also, try visualising yourself in a fearful situation. If you fear doing a psychic reading for a friend because they will laugh at your mistakes, then see yourself facing this scenario. Remind yourself, 'Is that all I have to worry about, them laughing at me? It doesn't mean I'm not psychic.' Reinforce the belief that you are indeed gifted, that the sixth sense is within all of us.

Now visualise a lovely yellow light forming a manifestation bubble in your solar plexus area. State your intention, 'I have the sixth sense. I trust in my abilities.' Visualise the bubble floating out to the universe. Ask that it manifest as a reality.

Re-ignite self-confidence by making a conscious choice to believe in *you*. How important is your dream? If you want it enough, infuse it with passion. Take action and create movement. You'll be surprised how easy it is moving through fear when you distract yourself by taking positive action. Practise self-confidence and remind yourself how wonderfully gifted you truly are.

59

More Than a Crystal Ball

Having confidence in your ability makes a world of difference. It can help you reach unimaginable heights. But despite all of this, occasionally the sixth sense goes off line.

There's nothing worse than feeling completely blocked, but it's perfectly natural to go through periods like this, and even the most talented psychics and mediums have bad hair days. Some of the reasons we get psychically blocked include lingering self-doubt, unresolved third eye chakra issues or being low on energy due to illness. Anything that lowers your personal vibration can definitely impact on the strength of your sixth sense.

There is also another reason why the sixth sense falters—you've hit a spiritual or energetic plateau. This often comes unexpectedly. One minute you're flying high and getting the most incredible information and insights, then suddenly nothing. It feels as if someone has pulled out your plug.

Don't take it to heart. We all experience a plateau at some stage. A plateau is a levelling point. Even though you feel as if you've psychically flat-lined for a day, or weeks, or occasionally even months, there's something very important going on. You're energetically levelling off—integrating all that you have been learning from working with the sixth sense. I like to think of it as pausing halfway up a mountain and thinking about how far you've come. Then, once you've realised this, things free up and you can continue walking up the mountain. In reality, you've just moved up another notch in your development. You'll find that after a plateau period that your sixth sense comes back with a vengeance, it's even stronger than before.

The key to working through plateau periods is to stay positive and keep trying to use your sixth sense, even if you feel or see nothing. When I've hit a plateau period I like to turn to my psychic tools for support. I introduce my students to psychic tools as a means of helping them to develop their sixth sense, but they are also a fantastic stimulus to work with while the sixth sense is being recharged.

Psychic tools include crystal balls, tarot, numerology, palmistry and astrology to name a few. What I love about psychic tools is that they offer a unique structure and process to help you get focused and find answers.

Crystal balls

When I was twenty-three I visited a psychic for a reading. When she pulled out a crystal ball my first thought was, 'You've got to be kidding!' How could any serious psychic see things in a crystal ball? I was judging something I didn't understand. I didn't know that crystals are natural amplifiers. There's nothing magical about them, but they really do help psychics to focus.

And that's what tuning in is all about. Peering into a crystal ball gives a focal point and helps you shut out interference from the rational mind. The intuitive mind can switch on and tune in. You don't actually see visions in the crystal ball; it just helps you get impressions in your psychic eye. It's certainly worth a try.

Tarot

The tarot is a beautiful tool for predicting the future. It's an intricately linked system of seventy-eight symbolic cards that tell a story. It can be used to look at what's coming up for you and you can also use it as a tool to gain self-awareness. Either way, the tarot has a wonderful way of helping us get answers when we hit a crossroad and need to make important decisions.

The tarot works through symbolism to paint a picture of our life—what is going on within us, around us and what's waiting for us around the corner. A standard tarot deck consists of twenty-two major Arcana and fifty-six minor Arcana cards. The gifted psychologist Carl Jung saw the spiritual element in the cards and suggested that the first eleven major Arcana cards represent your personality and your journey into the outside world. The other eleven major cards explore the depths of the inner world that bring you to self-actualisation. Seen in this light the major Arcana represent the twenty-two paths to the self, the life stages we all pass through. This is why they're such an effective tool for self-awareness. The different spreads give you the perfect structure to build your reading around. At the risk of sounding clichéd the pictures on the cards really do paint a thousand words.

There's so many tarot decks on the market it can get confusing, especially because of the different themes, symbols and designs. I usually recommend the Universal Waite tarot because it is so simple to use. I find the archetypal symbols help you relax and focus, which means your sixth sense flows more freely.

Palmistry

The ancient Vedic tradition says that the lines on your palm never lie. The Vedic art of palmistry interprets the lines and mounts on your hands, the shape of your fingers and their flexibility etc, to assess where you are now in your life and to make predictions for your future. Every line on your palm reveals a different facet of your life. For example, the heart line, head line and life line all yield information regarding what's happened in your relationships, how your mind works and the key stages in your life. Your dominant hand reveals the present and what's coming up, while the non-dominant hand represents the past.

I remember visiting a well-known palmist. I didn't give him my surname because he had met my ex-husband a week earlier and would realise what business I was in. He began by making some accurate comments on my childhood. Then he said, 'Well, aren't you a psychic miss!'

'Where do you see that?' I asked, careful not to show any recognition.

He pointed to some prominent squares on my palm and said, 'In fact you're very, very psychic. You do this for a living don't you?'

Like any structured psychic tool, palmistry weaves together information on the past and how it has influenced personality and experiences, and how it can affect the future. Keep an eye on your palms and you'll see lines fade when something changes. For example, when a major relationship is finishing, the relationship lines actually begin to fade. When a new line appears it symbolises a new beginning in a particular area of your life.

Astrology

Astrology is a scientific discipline based on mathematics and the movement of planets in our solar system, so it is very technical and precise. The harmonic pull of each planet affects our lives. You could say that our inner-soul mechanics are hardwired to respond to the cosmic dance of planets. When certain planets move into particular relationships the alignments activate karma stored within our chakras, so it influences our physical, emotional, psychological and spiritual self by drawing harmonic energy that helps attract events and people into our circle. These energies also help us become self-aware.

Some of the best astrologers I've meet use their intuition. Even though most astrologers say they work scientifically, their intuition gives them a better feel and accuracy for their readings. For example, when two planets conjunct (meet together) there can be three or four ways to interpret the information. Working with the sixth sense helps the astrologer target the most appropriate expression of the alignment. I do a little astrology but I tend to do it less scientifically and much more intuitively and I find it gives me insights in many key life areas.

Numerology

Who would have thought numbers could be so interesting. And predictive! The numbers 1 to 9 and the cipher 0 have a unique essence, harmony, virtue and attributes and help define us. Based upon your date of birth, the numbers reveal your unique physical, emotional, psychological and spiritual patterns. The sequences of numbers in your numerology chart reveal your gifts and challenges and help you to understand your inner-self, your karma and destiny. In other words, your number sequences indicate what you need to add and subtract from your life in order to get the perfect equation.

The numbers work in cycles, so you can map out gifts and lessons for every year of your life. The universe operates in terms of cycles and patterns and just as the solar system moves in a pattern, your individual life is a sequence of patterns within a larger cycle. Numerology is an easy, fun and wonderful tool that can help you expand your sixth sense.

We all need a little help from time to time. It's marvellous to know there are lots of effective psychic tools on hand to help you when you need them most. Now you won't have to wrestle with yourself when you're feeling blocked. Each psychic tool has its own unique way of guiding you while you're wading through the plateau period.

60

Go to It!

Your sixth sense is real and science is slowly coming around to this realisation. The sixth sense is always working in the background, orchestrating subtle moves that influence who you connect with. It gives you a helping hand when you most need it, especially when it comes to meeting people who will be significant players in your life.

I've spoken about how your personal energy can affect other people, and how they can affect you; now imagine this: two strangers meeting and their brains physiologically connecting even though they're unaware of it at the time. According to an article published in the *Sun-Herald* (26 September 2010), neurophysiologist Trisha Stratford has researched how we unknowingly use our sixth sense to chat up potential partners. She looked at how we align with another person based on a sense of oneness which has been triggered by physiological concordance. The article suggested that in-tune couples are in sync—that the sixth sense somehow helps their brains synchronise. It was discovered that while they are in sync their nervous systems are beating harmoniously. Trisha was excited to find that during a moment of oneness, 'We can read each other's brains and bodies at a deeper level—a sixth sense.' I should point out this applies equally to partners who provide unhappy learning experiences.

Alan Meara, a psychotherapist supervising the research, added that sixth-sense knowing, 'is something that the human brain is wired to do.' It's a natural part of us. Incredible as it sounds, our sixth sense is doing its job and helping us draw in, connect and feel a sense of oneness with people who are meant to become a part of our lives.

I remember how I met Stephen. I was supposed to book in for an operation and the choices I had were either late November or early December. Something urged me to take the November date so I could make the company Christmas party. About three hundred guests attended the party but despite being surrounded by so many people, I managed to be drawn to his table. As we got talking something clicked in my brain and I immediately sensed a deeper connection and knew I had met someone significant. I know the sixth sense was steering me to where I needed to be and helping me connect with him, it was like my body's intuitive intelligence took over and it just knew what to do. I often connect with new friends and close work colleagues this way. I'm sure you have done this too.

Try looking back at the major events in your life and think for a moment how you managed to be where you were to meet your partners or other key people. Peel back the layers and you'll find that your sixth sense was involved in leading you to that place. You'll discover that both your higher selves already knew the two of you were meant to connect.

Your sixth sense influences your thoughts, feelings and behaviour so why not take advantage and work with it to your benefit? It can be a rewarding and gratifying process. In fact, it's life changing! Besides, it seems counter-productive to fight the very part of you that's hardwired into your psyche for a very good reason. It's time to go for it.

Finetuning

Here are some tips on working with the sixth sense:

CLEAR YOUR ENERGIES

Before opening up the sixth sense do a quick meditation to help clear away tension and stress. Use universal and earth energy to raise your personal vibration.

BELIEVE IN YOUR ABILITY

Self-doubt creates self-defeat. Lingering doubt blocks your intuitive ability because you get stuck in left-brain thinking. Remind yourself you have unique gifts.

QUIETEN YOUR MIND

Don't be distracted by erratic thoughts that pop into your head. Instead of attaching to them, let them float away and focus on tuning in.

RELAX

Maintain a sense of inner harmony while working with the sixth sense. It helps to keep your channel open.

TAKE YOUR TIME

Putting unnecessary pressure on yourself by expecting to get immediate answers won't help. The sixth sense is timeless. Relax and trust that the information will come through at its own pace.

CHILL OUT

Stress acts like quick-setting cement—it can block you in seconds. Don't let the thought of making mistakes stress you. Remember, we learn from mistakes!

FINETUNE

If you are feeling blocked during the middle of your intuitive focus, stop and relax. Don't struggle with the fact you're feeling blocked. Simply take in a deep breath and slowly exhale a few times until you feel relaxed. State your intention to reactivate the sixth sense. Visualise a lovely ray of indigo light washing down over you, slowly opening and expanding your intuition.

LET GO

Release any performance anxiety or apprehensions you're holding on to. People appreciate that you're trying to help them by giving them your valuable insights.

GO WITH THE FLOW

Trust that the right information will be given to you from Spirit and your higher self.

REWARD YOURSELF

Remind yourself that you are doing well. It may help to give yourself a little reward every time you push through a barrier. You deserve it!

61

Don't Forget the Frosting

Every time I met a partner it was an awe-inspiring moment where I was at a crossroad between fear, uncertainty, joy and discovery. I intuitively knew that I was experiencing something extraordinary. That's what I love about working with the sixth sense. It tells you what you need to know, like who is going to be important to you, what the future holds and where your destiny lies.

Melissa's sixth sense helped her when she most needed it. She was pregnant with her third child, when she had a reappearance of a tumour in her breast.

'I went to see my specialist and he asked me if I was happy with my pregnancy. I said, "Isn't there any way you can operate while I'm pregnant and still protect my baby?"

'"There is a small window of opportunity between twenty and thirty weeks to have the operation," he said. "But, if the tumour grows in size at any time, I'll have to remove it immediately. And I have to warn you that this could jeopardise your baby."

'I was feeling hugely burdened by this over the next days and weeks and thinking of how I needed to hold it all together for the sake of the baby and my two other children. Then a week before my next scheduled appointment with my specialist, I think I was about nineteen weeks, I checked for the tumour and it was still the same size. I remember getting a strong sixth sense impression that the only way to get out of this situation was for "the tumour to just disappear".

'I got a sense it would miraculously disappear. It was an intuitive, yet passing thought, and for a brief moment I felt calm and relieved.

'I wanted to believe it but then logic butted in and I started stressing out again. I wasn't into spiritual stuff back then and I didn't pray because I didn't believe that it would do anything, or that the situation could be changed. I just wanted to go to sleep and wake up with no tumour.

'The night before my specialist appointment I decided to check for the tumour and I couldn't find it. Maybe I was deluding myself because I really didn't want to have the operation. The following day I turned up for my appointment and my specialist asked, "How is it going? Are you ready to book the date for the surgery?"

'"I think it's gone." I said. "It was there last week but last night I couldn't feel the lump anywhere in my breast."

'He was sceptical. "Tumours don't disappear overnight." He examined me and exclaimed, "Well, yes it's gone!"

Melissa walked through the car park feeling stunned.

'"For goodness sakes Melissa," I told myself, "you should be jumping for joy, and celebrating." But this huge release was taking its time to sink in; not all celebrations are in the moment.

'I finally gave birth to a lovely, healthy little daughter. And guess what—she is now studying medicine. I'm sure that my medical drama while she was in utero inspired her dream to become a healer. And she also happens to be a medium!

'My death scare in pregnancy taught me that you have to have the mindset that anything is possible. It ended up being a gift because it gave me something I believed couldn't happen. In my crisis, I managed to intuitively tap into the mind–body connection and I got my miracle!'

I like to think of the sixth sense as a compass that will always point you in the right direction no matter which way you're facing. When you believe in your abilities—whether they are clairvoyance, clairaudience, clairsentience or mediumship, or trust in Spirit—you can confidently face the undulations of life. Don't take this beautiful gift for granted because it isn't a sensory organ that works all by itself. It's the orchestra of supportive light-beings working alongside you that makes your sixth sense such a unique and powerful gift. These guys have been with you every step of the way.

This notion hit home for me recently. Late Friday night my son Tristan and his friends did what kids their age do and decided to push the envelope by speeding towards a dangerous hairpin turn halfway down a mountain side. One wrong move could have landed them in oblivion. About five hundred metres from the hazardous spot Tristan's ears started ringing madly, so he tuned in.

'Slow down, you are going to have an accident,' his guide warned. Tristan knew the driver wouldn't listen (youths often think they're invincible) so he asked his guide to help him.

'I'm still freaked out about it,' he confessed to me the following day. 'My guide surrounded the car in a green light. I could see it and feel it. Then suddenly the gears got stuck in second gear and the car slowed down. We ended up going around the hairpin turn in second gear! And we had to crawl all the way home in second gear too.'

I smiled and thanked his guides for putting disaster on hold. I know that some miracles do defy logic and are not everyday events but it doesn't mean they don't happen. And I'm so thankful for this one! Why not spend a moment giving thanks to your Spirit helpers for their exceptional advice and care? A little bit of gratitude goes a long way.

It's in the things that we can't explain, like premonitions and paranormal experiences, that we find strength, courage, insight and wisdom. This is because they open you up to a whole new way of looking at life. You have the sixth sense. It is your inner knowing, the part of you that's capable of making the right choice at the right time. It is your extra-sensory perception that helps you to 'read' people and situations clearly, communicate with loved ones in Spirit and even peer into the future. When you work with your sixth sense magic can happen. I have an unshakeable faith in the sixth sense and hopefully you do too.

Whenever I'm asked, 'Why do you work with the sixth sense?' I reply, 'Because it makes perfect sense.'